A COMMENTARY ON THE

Gospel

OF

Mark

A COMMENTARY ON THE

Gospel

OF

Mark

Terence J. Keegan, O.P.

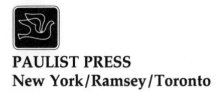

PAULIST PRESS
New York/Ramsey/Toronto

Copyright © 1981 by
Terence J. Keegan, O.P.

Library of Congress
Catalog Card Number: 81-82332

ISBN: 0-8091-2359-2

Published by Paulist Press,
545 Island Road, Ramsey, N.J. 07446

Printed and bound in the United States of America.

Contents

Preface

Mark's Gospel is unique in many ways. It is the shortest Gospel. It has the least amount of material not found in any other Gospel. It was the first Gospel to be written. Finally, and sad to say, through most of the history of Christianity it has been the least read and commented upon.

The reason for Mark's unpopularity is simple. Most people read the Gospels with an interest in the stories about Jesus. Since the other Gospels contain more information, people naturally read these fuller accounts. It is not that people are or ever have been biased against Mark. It is rather the case that people generally pay little attention to the Gospel's author, whoever he may be, and simply read the accounts that contain the stories of interest to them.

Until recently biblical scholars treated Mark with the same benign neglect as the general lay reader. About a century ago the realization that Mark's was the earliest Gospel generated some scholarly interest. However, scholars became interested only in Mark's Gospel as a record of traditions about Jesus, but not in Mark the writer. Well into our own century Mark, like the other evangelists, was regarded by critical scholars as little more than a compiler of traditions.

More recently scholars have realized that the evangelists were much more than recorders. They were theologians, each of whom had a unique insight into the mystery of salvation. This scholarly awareness actually accords well with a correct understanding of inspiration. Each of the Gospel writers was enlightened by the Holy Spirit and guided by that same Spirit to set down in writing words that would nourish the Church throughout the ages.

It would be impossible to determine which of the Gospels is most important. All four are important, but each one is unique. Each evangelist has something important to say to us if we are willing to be patient, to read and to listen. Even though Matthew and Luke reproduce over ninety percent of the material in Mark, we can only hear what Mark has to say by reading Mark, i.e., by recognizing from the outset that even though the stories may sound the same the message of each evangelist is unique and special. Furthermore, we can only hear what Mark has to say if we allow ourselves to be guided in our reading by the same Spirit that guided Mark's writing.

This commentary, then, is designed to explore the mind and message of Mark the inspired writer. Mark had a deep understanding of the message of salvation, an understanding that developed out of the lived experience of Christianity in the first generation after Jesus. About the year 65 A.D. Mark set down in writing, first for the Christians of his own day but also for Christians of every day, this unique understanding. Through careful study and using the best of contemporary biblical research we will attempt to penetrate the meaning of his Gospel for us. The purpose of this commentary, then, is twofold: first, to analyze Mark's Gospel and uncover, for the general reader, the purpose and plan of Mark's Gospel and the message he tried to convey; second, to open up the message of Mark's Gospel in a way that has meaning for our lives as Christians today.

While this book may be used effectively by individuals interested in studying Mark, it has been designed primarily for group study. The reasons for this group orientation are twofold. First, group discussions can often open up dimensions of meaning that individual study will miss and can also be an effective means of relating the Gospel to everyday life. Second, the Gospels themselves were written for community use and actually came into being as a result of the early Christians sharing their faith experience of the Good News of salvation.

A recommended use of this book, then, would involve individual readers first reading portions of the Gospel and commentary alone under the guidance of the Holy Spirit. After careful reflection on the meaning of the passages, a group would come together to share their individual insights and collectively apply the Gospel message to their daily lives.

The text of Mark on which this commentary is based is taken from *Good News for Modern Man* (Today's English Version). Unless otherwise noted, all New Testament quotations are taken from Today's English Version, while all Old Testament quotations are taken from the Revised Standard Version.

As I conclude I would like to thank all those who have helped me with this book: first, my students at Providence College whose interest, enthusiasm and probing questions powerfully aided the development of this book; second, my typists, Mrs. Cheryl Guglielmi who read my writing and typed the manuscript, and Mrs. Claire Greene, my aunt, who also assisted with the typing; finally, Miss Maryann Kolakowski, a graduate student who read the manuscript and suggested many clarifying improvements. Without the help of these and others this book would not have been completed.

Chapter One

SUMMARY. In this first chapter we will look at the first thirty-nine verses of Mark's Gospel. Mark does not, like Matthew and Luke, begin with the birth of Jesus. Instead he begins by showing how the Good News of salvation appeared on the scene as the fulfillment of the expectations of Israel.

These verses serve as an overture to Mark's Gospel, for in them Mark summarizes the main themes of the entire Gospel. The Good News is first realized in Jesus, God's Son. Jesus proclaims this Good News both in his preaching and in his miracles, he calls disciples to follow him in the realization of the Good News, and he goes to Galilee to bring the Good News to all mankind.

The Good News of salvation is God's gift to us, but, as we shall see, it is a gift that calls forth the response of repentance and faith. Mark's Gospel then is both a story and a challenge. As we read Mark's Gospel we should constantly be asking ourselves: "How am I responding to the challenge of the Good News?"

READ 1:1–39

OVERVIEW. What is *a* Gospel? What is *the* Gospel? The Good News of salvation arrived in the person and ministry of Jesus. A generation later Mark set out to tell the story of this Good News by creating a new kind of literature, a Gospel. After another generation Matthew, Luke and John followed Mark's lead by composing the other three canonical Gospels.

The Good News had come and had been proclaimed by a generation of preachers, but Mark was the first to set down in writing the full story of this Good News. In these first thirty-nine verses he explains what it is that he is doing, how the Good News came to be and in what it essentially consists.

A. APPEARANCE OF THE GOOD NEWS, 1:1–13

1. Good News, 1:1

If we were to write a biography of some famous person, e.g., George Washington, we might open with words such as these:

This is the story of George Washington. He began his life in . . .

The similar fashion in which Mark opens his Gospel indicates that he is not writing a biography of Jesus but rather a biography of the Good News about Jesus.

This is the Good News about Jesus Christ, the Son of God. It began . . . (1:1).

Though Mark will use the life and ministry of Jesus to tell his story, the subject of his story is the Good News itself. Recognizing this fact, we can appreciate more fully the meaning of Mark's Gospel and will not be disappointed if it does not measure up to our expectations of what a biography of Jesus should be.

The many incidents from the life of Jesus which Mark uses were incidents that were remembered and retold by a generation of Christians as they proclaimed, experienced and shared the Good News. Even more important than the details of the stories themselves are the reasons why these stories were remembered and retold, i.e., how they helped the early community to understand and explain the Good News.

When something funny happens in our own experience we remember it because it was funny. We retell it because it will bring laughter and merriment to our friends. Incidents from the life of Jesus were remembered because of their significance for what Jesus has done for us. They were retold in the early Christian community to fulfill a specific need of that community, e.g., preaching, teaching, liturgy.

When we find these stories in Mark's Gospel the most important consideration is why Mark used them. Mark, in telling the story of the Good News, follows a well thought out plan. Everything he includes serves, in some way, the general purpose of his Gospel. By understanding not only the meaning and significance of each incident he relates but also the role that this incident plays in Mark's Gospel as a whole, we can grasp even better the full meaning of Mark.

2. From John to Jesus, 1:2–11

OVERVIEW. According to Luke's Gospel, John the Baptist was the son of Mary's cousin Elizabeth and was born just a few months before Jesus. Mark, however, tells us nothing about the births of either John or Jesus. Instead he tells us about the emergence of the Good News in a manner quite parallel to the birth of a child.

Just as a woman's pregnancy is a sign, clear to anyone, that a child is soon to be born, so also the preaching of John the Baptist was a sign that the Good News of salvation was about to appear. In the climactic moment of childbirth the mother, in joyful pain, surrenders the fruit of her womb and a new, autonomous, human existence begins. Likewise a climactic moment is reached when John's ministry is completed and the ministry of the one bringing the Good News of salvation begins.

a. Ministry of John, 1:2–8

The people of the Old Testament lived in constant expectation of salvation, awaiting the one who would be sent by God to save his people. Many prophets, speaking God's word, had assured the people that salvation would come and had indicated the signs by which they could recognize the approach of salvation. Mark begins by quoting from these prophets to show that the preaching of John was precisely what had been foretold as a sign of the appearance of salvation.

> *John appeared in the desert, baptizing people and preaching his message. "Turn away from your sins and be baptized" (1:4).*

John is considered by many to be the last of the Old Testament prophets, for like all the prophets before him he spoke God's constant appeal to his people to turn away from sin and back to him (Is 31:6; Jer 3:22; Ez 14:6). Despite all the appeals of the prophets, despite all the marvelous manifestations of God's power in the lives of his people, they did not turn back to God (Am 4:6–11). They did not turn because they could not, by themselves, turn. The power of sin had entered human affairs and would not be banished until the savior sent by God should appear. Now, as the moment of salvation approached, John, the last of the prophets, issued this final call for turning away from sin and urged the people to symbolize this turning in baptism.

Water is the most frequently used symbol in the Old Testament. It symbolizes both death, as in the deluge (Gn 7:17–24), and life, as in the waters of Meriba (Ex 17:6–7). The most powerful uses of this symbol, however, occur when it is used to signify both death and life as in the waters of the Red Sea (Ex 14:21–31). When the Hebrew nation passed through these waters they ceased being a people in bondage and became God's own people. The waters of baptism have this double significance. Entering into the waters one dies to one's former way of life; emerging from the waters one rises to a new life. John's baptism, however, was only partial; it was only preparatory. John's baptism symbolized turning away from sin, dying to that state of bondage to sinfulness. The new life that would emerge was about to appear with Jesus.

> *I baptize you with water, but he will baptize you with the Holy Spirit (1:8).*

John, as the last of the prophets, was announcing the end of an age and the approaching dawn of a new age. Just as Jesus will shortly proclaim the arrival of God's Kingdom in both word and deed, John announced his message both by what he said and what he did. His bizarre behavior, living in the desert, dressed in camel's hair and eating locusts and wild honey, all symbolized his conviction that the world into which he was born, with all of its values, customs and comforts, was coming to an end. His behavior demonstrated his total rejection of all that the former age had to offer as he awaited the dawn of a new age. His behavior served to intensify his urgent message:

Turn away from your sins and be baptized (1:4).

b. Baptism of Jesus, 1:9–11

In his preaching in the desert John had prepared his followers for the one who would come after him and be greater than he was. Now, in the final act which Mark records about John's desert ministry, Jesus emerges from the waters of baptism as the first one to live the new life of God's Kingdom.

The people from nearby Jerusalem were coming out to the desert to hear John and be baptized, but Jesus came all the way from Nazareth in Galilee. The distance is only about sixty miles (as the crow flies) but when travelling on foot through rugged hills and jagged wastelands it would be a far greater distance and require a journey of several days. Galilee, as we shall see when we discuss 1:14, is quite important for the theological orientation of Mark's Gospel. Here, however, it is significant to note that Jesus was not a casual passerby who saw a crowd and decided to find out what was happening. Rather, he made a deliberate and arduous journey to a point in time and space where the Old Law and the New Law would meet. It is not without significance that tradition locates this site in that region of the Jordan where Joshua first led God's people out of the wilderness and into the Promised Land.

John baptized Jesus just as he had baptized so many others. As with the others Jesus' baptism symbolized death to the former age, the age of Satan, the power of sin. Jesus' baptism, however, was much more, for something unique happened as he emerged from the water. Jesus' baptism symbolized not only death to all that is evil but also newness of life, a life that comes from the

Spirit of God, a life that is most fully expressed by the simple words: "You are my own dear Son" (1:11).

c. Son of God, 1:11

Children are like their parents. For better or for worse, after the trauma of adolescence, men and women usually emerge into adulthood pretty much the same as their parents. They have similar tastes, similar talents and similar faults. Children of musicians often become musicians just as children of child beaters often become child beaters. God's will for his people had been written in the Law of Moses and announced time and again by the prophets but the people could not live according to God's will. They were born into sinful humanity; they were sinners and, in a sense, children of Satan. Jesus is the first who is not a child of Satan. As he emerged from the waters of baptism God acknowledged him as his own dear Son.

"Son of God" is a powerful concept which Mark uses to present the full reality of the Good News. Mark uses this concept to teach us not only who Jesus really is but also who we are in relation to Jesus. Paul had given expression to this same idea in his letter to the Romans:

> *Those whom God had already chosen he had also set apart to become like his Son, so that the Son would be the first among many brothers (Rom 8:29).*

Mark also uses the concept "Son of God" to aid in the structure of his Gospel. We will explain this usage when we consider 1:25. Here, however, let us notice a significant difference between Mark and Matthew in the words spoken by the voice from heaven.

Matthew 3:17	Mark 1:11
This is my own dear Son, with whom I am well pleased.	You are my own dear Son. I am well pleased with you.

The words in both are almost identical but in Matthew they are spoken *about* Jesus, probably being addressed to and heard by

John and those with him. In Mark, however, they are spoken *to* Jesus and there is no indication that anyone other than Jesus heard them.

What actually happened, what actually was heard and by whom we cannot know. Certainly neither author was present at the event. Both agree on the main substance of an event that was remembered and retold in the early Christian community. Each, however, adapts the story to suit the particular theological purpose it is intended to serve in the context of his own Gospel. For Mark, as we shall see, it is of great importance that until almost the end of his Gospel no human other than Jesus himself knows that he is the Son of God.

HISTORICAL ACCURACY

Let us digress a little here and discuss the question of historical accuracy. Granting that Mark is retelling stories that were being retold in the early Christian community and granting that he picks and chooses among these stories according to his theological purpose, we can still ask: Did it really happen that way? Is it historically true?

This question is often raised because of the many differences to be found in the accounts of the four Gospels. When we notice that Matthew and Mark record words differently or that Mark and Luke have Jesus performing the same miracle in different places we can only conclude that the historical facts have been obscured.

Here, however, we are raising a question (historical accuracy) that is peculiar to our own age and mentality and would not have occurred to the Gospel writers of the first century. Nevertheless, it is the consensus of most scholars that of all the evangelists Mark is the closest to the historical facts.

Recall the example of the funny event that is remembered and retold. The event actually happens. It is remembered and retold, but as it is passed on by word of mouth over a period of time the story often changes. Details of time, place and persons present tend to vary or become obscure. What remains constant is that aspect of the event that was funny and continues to cause laughter and merriment. The rest of the details are of lesser significance and can easily change as the story is retold.

The further removed a story becomes from the actual event the more likely it is that non-essential details will have changed or disappeared altogether. When we look at the stories about Jesus, then, those versions that contain the greatest incidence of non-essential detail are likely to be the closest to the original event. This situation is exactly what we find in Mark's Gospel. When we consider the miracle of the Gerasene demoniac, for example (Mk 5:1–20; Mt 8:28–34), we will see how both agree on the main substance of what Jesus did in driving the demons out of the man. Mark's version, however, is full of the kind of precise detail that would indicate it is very close to an eyewitness account.

Although Mark is named in five New Testament books we do not know if any of these refer to the author of our Gospel or even if they all refer to the same person, for Mark was a relatively common name. The certain identity of Mark will remain unknown but there is an ancient tradition which maintains that he was a companion of Peter. The vivid, eyewitness character of this Gospel, then, would have come from no less a person than the first of the apostles.

More recently it has been suggested that Mark himself may have been an eyewitness to at least some of the events of Jesus' life. Recall how it was stressed earlier that everything Mark relates fits into the purpose and structure of the Gospel as a whole. We therefore have to ask of each passage not only what it means in itself but also why Mark uses it, why he places it in a particular position, how it serves the purpose of the Gospel as a whole.

There is a curious incident related in 14:51–52 about a young man who ran away naked from Gethsemane. Some scholars, unable to find any other plausible explanation for the incident, have suggested that the young man was none other than the author of this Gospel. Possibly he used this incident to autograph his work just as Alfred Hitchcock in our own century would autograph his movies by appearing in them himself.

Exactly who Mark was or whether or not he was an eyewitness we cannot be certain. We are certain, however, that the author of this Gospel was a unique person singled out by the Spirit at the close of the first apostolic generation and guided by that same Spirit in composing our first written account of the Good News of salvation. The guarantee of the Spirit renders this work far more valuable to us than any proof of historical accuracy.

3. Temptation of Jesus, 1:12–13

Jesus is God's Son. He is the first one truly able to do God's will. The moment of salvation has arrived. The Kingdom of Satan is drawing to an end and the arrival of the Kingdom of God is about to be announced. Before Mark has Jesus proclaim the Good News of the Kingdom, however, he shows us something of the mysterious nature of this Kingdom in the story of Jesus' temptations.

The "Kingdom" concept used in the Gospels is somewhat similar to the "Son" concept discussed earlier. Back in the days when kings exercised real power a kingdom was a place, a well-defined geographical area, where the will of the king determined what could and could not be done. The king had the final say in all matters, legislative, executive or judicial. If a person did not like the laws of the king he could leave. He could, for example, cross the Pyrenees from France into Spain. Once in Spain, however, he would be under the rule of the king of Spain.

The Kingdom of Satan is that sphere of human existence where Satan rules, where things are the way Satan wants them to be, where sin abounds and results in sickness and death. The Kingdom of God, on the other hand, is that sphere of human existence where God rules, where things happen the way God has always wanted them to happen. Sons of God have turned away from Satan's Kingdom and entered God's Kingdom. Unfortunately, entering God's Kingdom is not as simple as crossing the Pyrenees into Spain and saying good-bye forever to the Kingdom of France.

The story of the temptation shows us that even in God's Kingdom the influence of Satan can still be felt. Jesus is God's Son. The moment of salvation has arrived. Jesus follows the guidance of the Spirit, goes to the desert and there encounters Satan. Does this mean that Jesus is not God's Son? Does this mean that the Kingdom of God has not really arrived? Certainly not! What it does mean is that the reality of God's Kingdom is a mysterious reality that has a twofold aspect. The Kingdom of God is *already* here and at the same time *not yet* here.

Jesus, as God's Son, has brought into the world the possibility for all of us to become God's children, doing his will and living in his Kingdom. Though we may be God's children, however, we still live in the context of sinful humanity. We still encounter the rule of Satan all around us and even within us. The significance of the story of the temptations of Jesus is that our simultaneous presence in the Kingdoms of God and Satan should not unsettle us, for Jesus himself had the same experience. What Mark will make clear as his Gospel progresses is that while God's Kingdom is firmly established, Satan's Kingdom is coming to an end. We can be confident, then, that we are children of God living in his Kingdom as we await the day when the Kingdom of Satan will be completely destroyed.

B. JESUS PROCLAIMS THE GOOD NEWS, 1:14–39

OVERVIEW. The first half of Mark's Gospel (1:14—8:26) can be divided into four parts which progressively develop the nature of the Good News. This first section (1:14–39) presents the fundamental reality of the Good News of salvation, the Kingdom of God. The second section (1:40—3:6) will bring out further aspects of this Kingdom by showing how it conflicts with the Judaism of Jesus' day. In the third section (3:7—6:6) Mark focuses on the identity of those who live in God's Kingdom, i.e., the true family of Jesus. Each of these three sections includes a call to discipleship (1:16–20; 2:13–14; 3:13–19). The fourth section (6:6—8:26) begins with the mission of the twelve (6:6–13) but its principal focus will be on their failure really to understand Jesus.

Throughout this Gospel the disciples are used by Mark as examples, both in their failures and in their successes, to aid us in realizing true discipleship. All of the other characters portrayed in this Gospel—Pharisees, Herodians, Sadducees, lawyers, tax collectors, prostitutes, foreigners—are similarly used to illustrate mankind's reaction to and relation to God's Kingdom.

1. Good News, 1:14–15

The climactic moment has been reached. Jesus, the Son of God, has appeared on the scene. In him the Kingdom of God, in its mysterious already and not yet nature, has been realized. Now Mark can describe the birth of the Good News by presenting Jesus proclaiming, for all to hear, the Good News first realized in himself.

Before stating that Jesus proclaimed the Good News Mark makes two preliminary comments. First, John the Baptist is imprisoned. Jesus begins his ministry only after the ministry of John has ended, just as the newborn child is first heard only after the term of pregnancy has ended. Second, Jesus returns to Galilee. Galilee, as mentioned earlier, is very significant for the theological orientation of Mark's Gospel. Jesus comes from Galilee. It is in Galilee that he first proclaims the Good News. It is to Galilee that he goes for his final encounter with the apostles after the resurrection.

North of Judea was Samaria where people considered to be apostates from true Judaism lived. North of Samaria was Galilee, a region populated by Jews who were looked down upon by the Jews of Judea, since the Galileans were not, for the greater part, descendants of Abraham. After the fall of the northern kingdom in 722 B.C. Israelites remained numerous in Samaria but Galilee became almost entirely populated with Gentiles. Even before 722 Galilee had a large Gentile population, for it is referred to by Isaiah as "Galilee of the nations" (Is 9:1). About a century before the birth of Jesus, during the reign of the Hasmonean kings, Galilee was incorporated into the Jewish kingdom and its inhabitants were forcibly converted to Judaism. The Judaizing of Galilee progressed and endured due to the settling of Jewish immigrants from Judea. Nevertheless, Galilee and the Galileans were never quite as Jewish as Judea. Matthew and Luke are very careful to show that Jesus was a descendant of David and therefore a descendant of these recent Jewish immigrants.

Mark, while recognizing that Jesus is descended from David (see 10:47–48), is more interested in Galilee precisely as Galilee of the nations. Salvation had been promised by God to his chosen people. It is first realized in Jesus himself in a mysterious already and not yet way. It is proclaimed by him to his own people but it is intended for all mankind. It is also intended to achieve its full realization when every trace of the Kingdom of Satan shall be removed. For Mark, Galilee becomes an open-ended symbol of this outward extension of the Good News, a spatial extension embracing all peoples and a temporal extension pointing to the not yet of the Kingdom.

It is in Galilee, therefore, that the proclamation of the Good News of salvation is first heard. Mark begins his presentation of the nature of this Good News by giving his readers a brief, summary glimpse of this new reality. The words of Jesus recorded in 1:15 probably are not an actual quote. If they were a quote they would have constituted one of the shortest sermons in history. These words are more likely a summary statement of the basic content of the Good News which Jesus proclaimed in many and varied ways all over Galilee.

This summary statement of the Good News consists of four parts, each of which brings out an essential aspect of the Good News.

The right time has come	Turn away from your sins
The Kingdom of God is near	Believe in the Good News

The two statements on the left are indicative, statements of fact. The two on the right are imperative, urgent appeals to do something. This juxtapositioning of indicative and imperative is another indication of the already and not yet nature of the Kingdom. God has already done something. The Kingdom is an accomplished fact. The translation we are using (TEV) is not as forceful in bringing out the accomplished nature of the Kingdom as is the Revised Standard Version (RSV), "the kingdom of God is at hand." Even though the Kingdom is accomplished, something still remains to be done by us to bring it about, turning and believing.

REPENTANCE

The two statements on top, "the right time has come" and "turn away from your sins," are a restatement of the appeal of John the Baptist: Salvation is now available so turn away from your sins. Most versions of the New Testament translate this appeal as "repent" but our version (TEV) brings out the precise meaning of repentance with its fuller translation, "turn away from your sins."

Too often we think of repentance as sorrow for our sinfulness. Repentance does involve sorrow but it also involves much more. It is rather easy and quite common to be sorry for the unfortunate consequences of our actions. I am sorry when I am caught speeding on the highway, but would I be sorry if I were not caught? I am sorry when my careless tongue offends people or causes them harm, but am I sorry for my tongue or merely for its consequences? Too often our sorrow is mostly external whereas true repentance is internal. True repentance involves recognizing that something is wrong with me and not just with the things that happen outside of me. True repentance involves turning, i.e., changing the course of one's existence.

The greatest difficulty involved in repentance is finding a new course for our lives. It is much easier to make minor adjustments in our present course than to search for and set out on a totally new course. John's preaching of repentance ended with repentance. He urged his followers to turn away from their former course but was unable to provide them with a new course. The two statements on the bottom, "the Kingdom of God is near" and "believe in the Good News," are Jesus' unique addition to John. Jesus not only calls us to repentance but he also provides us with a ready-made course for our new lives, the Kingdom of God as an accomplished fact. Now it is possible to live our lives according to the will of God. One thing only is required of us: that we believe in the Good News.

FAITH

Belief or faith, as we shall see, is a constant theme throughout Mark's Gospel. He will use the disciples and their difficulty in arriving at true faith as models for us in an attempt to aid us in reaching this true faith. Faith involves much more than facts or truths which cannot be demonstrated or seen. Most of all, faith involves persons. If I believe that, in my absence, a certain event happened, e.g., the president telephoned my home, I accept the fact but I accept it because of the person who told it to me. I believe because I trust that person, because I have a personal relationship with that person which makes it impossible for me not to believe. This personal relationship of trust is what Jesus is asking for. The Kingdom of God has come in the person and ministry of Jesus. The Kingdom of God will come in our lives if we enter into a personal relationship of trust with Jesus.

The prophet Isaiah focused on an important aspect of faith in a warning he once spoke to King Achaz. The Hebrew word Isaiah used to convey this aspect of faith is the word from which we get our expression "Amen," a word which literally means "to stand on." At the time of Achaz both Israel and Syria were about to wage war on Judah. Achaz wanted to seek the aid of Assyria, but Isaiah urged him to trust in God and not in earthly princes. He sternly warned him:

If you do not take your stand on God you shall not stand at all (Is 7:9).

Belief involves a risk. Whenever I believe a person I risk something, however small or insignificant it might be. Risk is involved because my life will somehow be affected by my choosing and acting in accord with my belief, e.g., when a friend assures me that he has tested the brakes on my car and they are safe. If I have faith in a person I am willing to take whatever risk is involved because of our personal relationship of trust. Jesus is asking us to take a risk, a rather incredible risk. He is asking us to turn away from taking our stand on self-centeredness and the security offered by the world and to take our stand on him. He is asking us to stake our lives, our entire existence on him. Only in this way can we truly live in God's Kingdom where everything is the way God wants it to be.

2. Discipleship, 1:16–20

The Kingdom of God, for me, involves my personal relationship of trust with Jesus. The perfect realization of the Kingdom involves all mankind entering into that relationship of trust. Being a disciple of Jesus, then, involves both faith in Jesus and living that faith in such a way that others will be brought to faith. It is significant that the first disciples called by Jesus were fishermen, for their lives as disciples would involve their drawing men out of their former manner of life and into a faith relationship with Jesus.

Calling disciples is the first activity of Jesus recorded by Mark because it is the primary reason why Jesus came into this world. He did not come to work miracles. He did not come to teach. He did not even come to die on the cross. These are all subordinated to his primary purpose, to draw all men to himself. Jesus' call to the first disciples is "Come with me" (1:17). He does not say for how long he wants them to be with him, but it will emerge in the course of the Gospel that the term of Christian discipleship is forever.

Many teachers of Jesus' day gathered disciples around themselves. A characteristic of all other teacher-disciple relationships was that discipleship was temporary. The ideal situation was for a disciple to learn all that a teacher had to offer and then become independent of him, becoming perhaps a teacher himself with his own disciples. Christian discipleship is unique, for a Christian never becomes independent of Jesus, his teacher.

3. Teaching by Word, 1:21–22

Like John before him, Jesus taught both by what he said and by what he did. Mark tells us here that Jesus taught by word, but he provides us with much less of the content of Jesus' teaching than do the other evangelists. When he does detail Jesus' teaching it is almost always in the second half of his Gospel (after 8:27). In the first half he teaches primarily by what he does or in parables, both techniques being a veiled form of teaching. Mark's approach is the result of the manner in which he will gradually unfold the full reality of the Good News.

Whether Jesus is teaching by word or by deed his teaching results in amazement on the part of those who hear and see. They are amazed because he is so unlike the rabbis of their day. The rabbis taught on the authority of Moses. Jesus teaches on his own authority as Son of God, just as he casts out evil spirits and heals the sick on that same authority. Even when he was simply teaching by word, however, it was clear that he was claiming an authority possessed by no one else of his day.

4. Teaching by Deed, 1:23–34

OVERVIEW. The first half of Mark's Gospel is devoted largely to showing Jesus exercising his authority to perform miracles. Here, in the first section, Mark presents the two kinds of miracles that demonstrate the fundamental nature of the Good News of the Kingdom.

In spite of his extensive treatment of miracles, a major objective of Mark's Gospel is to show that Jesus was not a miracle-worker. There were other people in Jesus' day who were regarded as miracle-workers. They performed marvelous feats, but the miracles they performed had no essential relationship to their purpose in performing them. They worked wonders for financial gain, for honor or simply to gain an audience for their teaching. Jesus, on the other hand, never performed a miracle to prove how great he was. He never performed a miracle to get people to listen to him. In everything he said and did, Jesus proclaimed the Good News of the Kingdom of God where the rule of Satan is ended and everything is the way God wants it to be. Mark, therefore, shows him driving out with authority things contrary to God's Kingdom.

a. Evil Spirit, 1:23–28

The most obvious aspect of the rule of Satan is his ability directly to influence and control the lives of people. Accordingly, the first miracle which Mark describes is an exorcism. Evil spirits, as powerful as they might be, are powerless when confronted with God's Kingdom. Because Jesus is God's Son, because in his person and in his presence things are as God wants them to be, the evil spirit loses control over the man and can do nothing but obey Jesus' command to come out.

This miracle story further supports the assurance Mark gave us in the story of Jesus' temptation. The rule of Satan is still very much in evidence in the world around us, but if we live in God's Kingdom, if we take our stand on Jesus, then evil spirits will be powerless in our presence. Temptations will continue to be part of everyone's life but they have no real power over one who lives by faith.

MESSIANIC SECRET

An important feature of this miracle story is the dialogue between the evil spirit and Jesus. The evil spirit knows that Jesus is "God's holy messenger" (1:24). Jesus responds to the evil spirit's cry with the command "Be quiet" (1:25). Here we have the first occurrence of what is called the messianic secret, a device used by Mark in structuring and developing his Gospel (see 1:34; 3:11–12; 5:7).

Apart from Jesus only the evil spirits know who he really is. They cannot help knowing the identity of him by whose authority their Kingdom is being annihilated. In Mark's Gospel, however, Jesus never acknowledges to anyone that he is God's Son, and he frequently commands the demons to keep quiet about his true identity. Mark uses this device of keeping Jesus' identity secret in order to unfold gradually the full reality of Jesus. One human will eventually recognize who Jesus is—the army officer at the foot of the cross. Looking upon Jesus and seeing in that moment the full reality of what he has done for us, the centurion exclaims: "This man was really the Son of God" (15:39).

b. Sickness, 1:29–31

In addition to the direct influence of evil spirits there are many other manifestations of the Kingdom of Satan in the world. None of the disorders in human existence, i.e., every kind of sin and certain kinds of sickness, were intended by God to be part of our lives. They entered in as a result of mankind's commitment to evil. In God's Kingdom, however, they cannot continue to exist. In the second miracle recorded by Mark, when Jesus heals Simon's mother-in-law, he eliminates sickness as a further proclamation in deed that the Kingdom of God has come.

Two features of this miracle story are especially noteworthy. First, when Mark wrote the phrase "helped her up" (1:31) he actually used the Greek verb which means "to raise up," the same verb he uses to describe Jesus' resurrection (see 14:28; 16:6). The use of this verb hints at the connection between Jesus' death and resurrection and our dying to the power of evil and rising to new life in God's Kingdom.

Second, we are told that after the fever left her she began to wait on them (1:31). Here the Greek verb Mark used is the word from which we get our word "deacon," which literally means "servant." Again Mark is telling this miracle story in such a way as to hint at the larger reality of how the Good News of the Kingdom is realized in us. First, we turn away from all that is evil and take our stand on Jesus. Second, we use the newness of life that Jesus has given us in the service of others.

c. Many Miracles, 1:32–34

In the final episode before the conclusion of this section Mark shows Jesus performing a multitude of miracles, healing many sick and driving out many demons (1:34). Wherever Jesus went and encountered demons he drove them out. Wherever, it seems, Jesus encountered sickness he healed it. Does this mean that all sickness is evil and we should expect the presence of God's Kingdom to overcome it? This question is troublesome for many today and Mark does not directly answer it. He does, however, give us one example in his Gospel of a person whose suffering was not overcome and who died—namely, Jesus.

Part of the solution would seem to lie in a distinction that might be made between "sickness" and "suffering." (The terms are in quotes because their literal meanings are slightly altered for the purposes of this distinction.) By "sickness" we can understand those afflictions which are contrary to God's plan for us, afflictions which stand in the way of God's Kingdom being fully realized in us. These are the kind of afflictions which Jesus healed. They are the kind that are cured today at Lourdes and wherever Christians invoke the power of God's Kingdom. By "suffering," on the other hand, we can understand those afflictions that are part of God's plan for us, afflictions which are present because of the conflict between the powers of good and evil, afflictions that can further the cause of God's Kingdom. Afflictions of this sort Jesus never encountered in anyone other than himself since they did not become part of Christian experience until after Jesus had first suffered, died and risen.

This distinction alone does not solve the problem, since there are many kinds of real sickness which do not fit in either category. Sickness of this sort is part of the normal course of human events, even those sicknesses which lead to death. Unfortunately Mark never tells us about Jesus encountering people with this kind of sickness, but we do have countless examples of people who have gone to Lourdes or to prayer meetings and returned home still sick. Many of these people, however, have returned home with the assurance that their lives, their eternal lives, are in God's hands, and they have lived out the remainder of their days as true witnesses to the reality of God's Kingdom.

5. Galilee of the Nations, the Beginning and the End, 1:35–39

The first section of Mark's Gospel concludes with a truly magnificent passage. This passage recapitulates the main ideas which have appeared up to this point: Jesus' relationship with God, "He went out of town to a lonely place, where he prayed" (1:35); the devotion of his disciples, "Simon and his companions went out searching for him" (1:36); Jesus' mission to proclaim the Good News, "I have to preach in them also" (1:38); and finally the Good News in action being proclaimed in word and deed, "preaching in the synagogues and driving out demons" (1:39).

This recapitulation serves as a fitting conclusion to this section (1:14–39) but what is truly magnificent about this passage is the way it anticipates the ending of the Gospel and together with that ending serves to hold the entire Gospel together as a single piece. Laid out below in parallel columns are the two passages, 1:35–39 and 16:2, 6. One cannot help noticing the remarkable similarity, especially in the phrases that have been italicized.

1:35–39	16:2, 6
Very early the next morning, long before daylight, *Jesus got up* and left the house. He went out of town *to a lonely place,* where he prayed. But *Simon and his companions* went out searching for him; when they found him they said, *"Everyone is looking for you."* But Jesus answered, "We must go on to the other villages around here. I have to preach in them also, because that is why I came." So he *travelled all over Galilee,* preaching in the synagogues and driving out demons.	*Very early on Sunday morning,* at sunrise, they went to the grave.... "Don't be alarmed," he said. *"I know you are looking for Jesus* of Nazareth, who was nailed to the cross. He is not here—*he has been raised!* Look, *here is the place* where they placed him. Now go and give this message to *his disciples including Peter:* 'He is *going to Galilee ahead of you;* there you will see him just as he told you.'"

Many of the similarities are quite incidental and serve only to link the two passages together, e.g., "very early the next morning," but other similarities are quite essential to the main thrust of Mark's Gospel. Simon and his companions are with Jesus at the beginning, they fare rather badly throughout the Gospel, as we shall see, but true to the nature of discipleship they are still there at the end.

Even more significant, perhaps, is the reference to Galilee. Jesus was baptized and crucified in Judea but the greater part of his ministry was carried on in Galilee. What Mark is emphasizing in linking these two passages together is that Jesus' ministry ended where it began with the open-ended symbol which is Galilee. Galilee, as we have indicated, symbolizes both an openness to all nations and an extension in time toward the perfect realization of the Kingdom. This temporal open-endedness is indicated by the suggestion that just as Jesus began his ministry in Galilee, the disciples after him will extend his ministry beginning in Galilee as well.

STUDY QUESTIONS

1. John the Baptist was prepared for the coming of salvation into the world. Are we prepared? What does the preaching of John and his manner of life mean for our lives?

2. In what ways are we already living in God's Kingdom? In what ways are we not yet living in God's Kingdom?

3. What do the temptations of Jesus mean for us today?

4. Can I describe the direction in which my life is moving? Is the direction of my life a source of difficulty for myself or those around me? What is the meaning and necessity of repentance for me?

5. How much of our daily lives is affected by faith in other people? How often are we afraid to rely on those around us? What does it mean for me to rely on Jesus? Am I comfortable with faith?

6. What is a miracle? Why did Jesus work miracles? Are miracles part of the present-day experience of the Church?

Chapter Two

CONFLICT WITH JUDAISM

Summary. Immediately after his overture to the story of the Good News, Mark shows Jesus proclaiming this Good News by his actions and words. In this chapter we will consider the manner of Jesus' proclamation, the message he proclaimed and the problems that arose.

Salvation had been promised to God's chosen people, the Israelites. The Jews of Jesus' day considered themselves to be the heirs of the promises first made to Abraham. Most, however, were unwilling to accept the salvation that Jesus brought.

Jesus began his ministry within the structures of first-century Judaism, preaching in synagogues and respecting all the customary observances. Jesus was not, however, the kind of savior people were expecting. He was not the kind of savior people wanted. When he did not fit into their plan for what they wanted God to do for them, they rejected him.

As we read this section we can ask ourselves what kind of preconceived ideas we have about what we want God to do for us. Would we too have rejected Jesus? Are we now rejecting Jesus?

READ 1:40–3:6

OVERVIEW. Jesus proclaims the Good News of the Kingdom of God by what he does, using his authority as Son of God to cast out everything that is contrary to God's Kingdom. In this second section of his Gospel Mark elaborates on the nature of the Good News by showing how the Kingdom proclaimed by Jesus' deeds is often in conflict with the Judaism practiced in his day. In addition, Mark relates several anecdotes in which these conflicts result in Jesus' making brief pronouncements that clarify further the nature of the Good News.

This section begins (1:40–45) and ends (3:1–6) with miracle stories. In between there are several pronouncement stories. The careful reader will notice here and elsewhere in Mark (and in the other Gospels as well) that most miracle stories follow the same basic outline. Pronouncement stories, likewise, have their own set outline.

A set outline for a given type of story is necessary for two reasons, the first of which we should all be able to appreciate. In our own day newspapers contain many kinds of material. On one page we read about a wedding, and before we read it we know what it will say. It will give the names of the couple, their parents and those in the wedding party, the place of the wedding, the colors of the gowns worn, etc. On another page we read about a football game. Again, we already know what information it will contain: the teams that played, the score of the game, the names of the players who scored and how they scored, etc. If a sportswriter dared to depart from the form of a football story and instead gave us the names of the coaches' parents and the colors of the assistant coaches' suits we would be thoroughly confused and would probably buy another newspaper. A set format, then, is necessary first of all for communication, for understanding. Each of the kinds of stories about Jesus had a set form. When the stories were told, people knew what to expect. They could then listen and understand.

The second reason for the necessity of a set format is perhaps more difficult to appreciate. These stories about Jesus were not, at first, printed in newspapers. They were passed along by word of mouth. The ancients did not have the resources for printing and reproducing that we have. Instead, they were far more capable than we at passing on material by word of mouth from one generation to the next. A tremendous aid to this oral transmission was the set outline. A miracle story that adhered to a set outline could far more easily be remembered and retold.

For a full generation stories about Jesus were cast into these set forms and handed on orally. Mark, in using these stories, sometimes adapts them according to his specific purpose in telling them but usually we can still see the clear outline of the form they followed while being transmitted orally.

A. A LEPER HEALED, 1:40–45

Miracle stories contain three basic elements: the circumstances in which the miracle occurs, an account of the actual miracle and the result of the miracle. The stories begin by introducing the affliction to be healed. Usually details are included which emphasize the difficulty of the case, e.g., the many doctors in the story of the woman with severe bleeding (5:26). In the second part of the story the actual cure is recounted detailing the physical routine or the commanding words used, e.g., spitting on the eyes of the blind man at Bethsaida (8:23). The final part of the story is some kind of a demonstration that a cure has been effected. The demonstration can be an action on the part of the one healed, e.g., Simon's mother-in-law waiting on them (1:31), or the confirmation of a third party, e.g., the examination by the priest in the story we are now considering (1:44).

All of these elements are present in this story of the cure of the leper, but, as mentioned in chapter one, what is most important is not the story itself as it was handed on orally but the specific purpose Mark intended it to serve in the development of his Gospel. Mark selected this story to serve as the introduction to his treatment of the conflict between the Good News and Judaism. He did so because the story contains a number of features which shed light on the relationship of the Good News to Judaism.

1. Person Healed

In the healing story of the previous section the person healed was Simon's mother-in-law. We have every reason to believe that she was a good, practicing Jew. The person healed in this story, however, was not. Lepers were not allowed to practice their religion. They were not even allowed to enter the temple precincts. A leper, according to Lv 13:45–46, was religiously unclean. In Jesus' day this religious impurity extended to anyone who encountered a leper or anything the leper touched. Unlike the prophet Elisha who cured Haaman the Syrian by having him wash in the Jordan (2 Kgs 5:10, 14), Jesus actually touched this leper (1:41). The Law of Moses could do nothing for lepers but exclude them from polite company. The Good News of God's Kingdom, however, knows no such limits; it extends to everyone, even outcasts.

2. Faith

The Kingdom of God has come but it is only real for me if I believe. Faith is an essential aspect of all the healing that takes place in God's Kingdom. Total, unqualified trust in Jesus, however, is hard to realize. Mark, as mentioned above, will use the disciples as examples of how hard it is to be true followers of Jesus. Mark's development of the role of faith in God's Kingdom begins in this story of the leper and reaches its high point in the story of the boy with an evil spirit which the disciples were unable to drive out (9:14–29). In that story Jesus exclaims to the father of the boy:

> "Everything is possible for the person who has faith." The father at once cried out, "I do have faith, but not enough. Help me have more!" (9:23–24).

Here in the story of the leper a kind of faith is present, a belief that Jesus can cure, but that perfect faith which involves a trusting relationship with Jesus is missing. The leper lacks confidence that Jesus will want to cure him. Jesus, however, responds to the faith that is present and assures the man that he does want to heal him. Having built a relationship of trust, Jesus effects the miracle with the command, "Be clean" (1:41).

3. Jesus' Attitude to the Leper and the Law

The attitude Jesus displays in this miracle story is markedly different from that which he will display in the story of the man with a crippled hand, the final miracle of this section (3:1–6). Here "Jesus was filled with pity" (1:41). There "Jesus was angry" (3:5). Here Jesus is careful to adhere to the requirements of the Law, sending the healed leper to be examined by the priest (1:41). There Jesus will alienate the Pharisees by refusing to observe the Sabbath as they would want him to (3:4).

Jesus' attitude is really consistent throughout. The apparent change is not in Jesus but in the growing opposition of those around him. Jesus' basic attitude toward those who were not enjoying the fullness of God's Kingdom was pity. Jesus, as God's Son, lived in his Kingdom and wanted all to share the riches of this Kingdom. When Jesus feeds the five thousand Mark tells us:

> His heart was filled with pity for them, because they were like sheep without a shepherd. So he began to teach them many things (6:34).

The pity Jesus felt for the leper is a pity he continues to feel for anyone and everyone who is lacking the fullness of his Father's Kingdom. Anger, as we shall see, is present in Jesus only when people have closed their minds and hearts to the possibility of entering God's Kingdom.

The Kingdom of God is where everything is the way God wants it to be. For over a thousand years before Jesus, through Moses and the prophets, God had been teaching his people his holy will. Even though his people were unable to observe this will because they were still in bondage to the powers of evil, many of them continued to study and transmit God's will in what we now know as the Old Testament. Jesus had great respect for the Old Law as the embodiment of God's will for his people, and he always showed this respect by carefully observing the requirements of the Law. In this story he shows this respect by sending the leper to the priest. Only when the observance of the Law comes into conflict with the will of God does Jesus disregard the Law.

How, one might ask, can the Law, which details God's will, come into conflict with God's will? There are actually two ways in which this conflict can arise. First, as Paul explains in his second letter to the Corinthians, the New Law is radically different from the Old Law.

> *It is written not with ink on stone tablets, but on human hearts, with the Spirit of the living God. . . . The capacity we have comes from God; it is he who made us capable of serving the new covenant, which consists not of a written law but of the Spirit. The written law brings death, but the Spirit gives life (2 Cor 3:3–6).*

Written laws are always inadequate. The real living experience of every human being is deeper and richer than any code of laws, even the written Law of God. The New Law, then, is written on the hearts of those who are God's children. It is a law that is adequate for every experience of the heart of man. It can come into conflict with the Old Law, then, because of the built-in limitations of any written law.

The second way in which God's will can come into conflict with the Law of Moses is similar to the first. Precisely because of the limitations of written laws they must constantly be interpreted and adapted for new situations. The teachers of the Law of Jesus' day were entrusted with this task of handing on the Law and interpreting it for the changing lives of the people. Unfortunately the teachers of the Law were not inspired as were Moses and the prophets, and often what they taught as the Law of God were really commands of men (see 7:8). Jesus' principal difficulties with the Law arose in this second way when the pure will of God conflicted with the Jewish practices of the day.

In the first story of this section, then, Mark shows Jesus bringing the Good News of God's Kingdom even to those beyond the reach of the Law while at the same time showing great respect for that Law. With this first story, however, Mark sets the scene for showing how Jesus' total commitment to God's Kingdom will inevitably conflict with the Judaism of the Pharisees.

4. Response of the Healed Leper

Jesus, as God's Son living in his Kingdom, brings the reality of God's Kingdom to all around him by what he says and what he does. He cannot do otherwise, for that would involve a denial of his divine Sonship. This truth is magnificently expressed in the fourth verse of a hymn contained in the second letter to Timothy. This verse, in a forceful and reassuring manner, breaks the parallelism of the first three verses.

If we have died with him,
    we shall also live with him.
If we continue to endure
    we shall also rule with him.
If we deny him
    he also will deny us.
If we are not faithful,
    he remains faithful
    because he cannot be false to himself (2 Tm 2:11–13).

What is true of Jesus is also true of those who have entered God's Kingdom, having become God's children. The experience of this new life is something one cannot keep to oneself. Somehow it must be expressed, witnessed and shared. In the words of Paul,

> *How terrible it would be for me if I did not preach the gospel! (1 Cor (9:16).*

When the healed leper began to spread the news everywhere he was responding as one touched by the power of God's Kingdom could not help responding. We saw in chapter one how Simon's mother-in-law witnessed to her being healed by serving those around her. The almost universal experience of those who have received what is called the "Baptism of the Holy Spirit" is that they cannot prevent themselves from talking about the wonderful source of life flowing through their entire being.

A problem we face in this story about the leper is that Jesus had ordered him not to tell anyone (1:44). This command which is repeated at the end of three other miracle stories (5:43; 7:36; 8:26) is related to Jesus' demand (discussed in chapter one) that the demons not reveal his true identity (1:25; 1:34; 3:11–12; 5:7). The reason for both of these demands is to be found in Mark's plan gradually to unfold the full reality of God's Kingdom. These two kinds of demands, however, differ in a number of significant ways.

The demons, on the one hand, know who Jesus really is. They have, however, been subdued by Jesus. Being powerless in the face of his authority they cannot disobey him. As a result only the demons and we the readers know who Jesus really is from the start. The various characters portrayed in Mark's Gospel, on the other hand, have only a limited and partial appreciation of who Jesus really is. Mark uses them in his plan of gradual unfolding and also uses them to warn us, the readers, not to settle for less than a full appreciation of who Jesus really is. The mistakes and failures of the leper and of all of these characters are meant as a warning to us that the full reality of Jesus and the Kingdom he announced is only made clear on the cross.

In the first half of Mark's Gospel Jesus is presented as a miracle-worker, but this is only a part of the full picture Mark wants to give us. The leper was following a natural response in spreading the news but he was leading many people, including the disciples, into a faulty understanding of who Jesus really was.

B. HOSTILITY OF THE PHARISEES, 2:1–28

The four stories which are contained in Mk 2 are all in the form of conflict pronouncement stories, notwithstanding the fact that the first of them includes an account of a miracle. They each begin by setting some kind of scene which includes the presence of people hostile to Jesus. Next, a dialogue is initiated which focuses on a need for a clear-cut answer. Finally, there is a statement by Jesus which resolves the conflict though it usually does not satisfy his enemies (2:10, 17, 19, 28).

In a pronouncement story what is most important is the statement by Jesus. This statement is the reason why the story was remembered and retold. The other elements in the story are of lesser significance and might be altered as the story was handed on by word of mouth. These stories, then, are quite different from miracle stories in which the actions of Jesus and the condition of the person for whom the miracle was performed are of primary importance.

Mark has selected these four pronouncement stories not only because Jesus' statements show how God's Kingdom is so radically new that it totally transcends the Judaism of his day but also because each of them brings out aspects of the meaning of Jesus' mission and the saving authority which is his as Son of God.

1. Cure of the Paralytic, 2:1–12

As mentioned above this story is really a pronouncement story. It was told because of the statement about the Son of Man having authority to forgive sins. The first part of this story is itself a genuine miracle story (notice the role of faith in 2:5) but here it serves the purpose of setting the scene for the conflict and subsequent pronouncement.

In the first half of Mark's Gospel the reality of God's Kingdom is unfolded primarily through what Jesus does rather than through what he says. In each of these four stories the opponents take offense at something that is done. Each time, Jesus' pronouncement shows that what was done is really in accord with the reality of God's Kingdom.

In this first story Mark shows Jesus doing what he had been doing from the beginning—performing a miracle for one whose life lacked the fullness which God had willed for him, in this case a man so paralyzed that he had to be carried about on a mat. Here, however, the commanding words by which Jesus effects the miracle point out a new dimension of God's Kingdom and also provoke, for the first time, the hostility of those around him:

My son, your sins are forgiven (2:5).

For the Jews of Jesus' day, major illness was regarded as a consequence of sin. This view is subject to serious misunderstanding but, in a sense, it represents a much more profound insight than does the modern medical view that many genuine physical ailments are psychosomatic in origin. What is involved in both of these insights is the relationship between surface symptoms and the root cause, e.g., anyone can treat the symptoms of a common cold but no one as yet seems to know how to eliminate the virus which causes the symptoms. Unless the root cause is eliminated the surface disorders will continue to reappear whether that root cause is a virus, a psychological deficiency or sin. What Jesus is doing in this miracle is eliminating the disorder at its root cause, showing that God's Kingdom is not simply a matter of band-aids and aspirin but involves a totally new beginning for man in perfect harmony with the will of God.

For the Jews of Jesus' day, sin was a disorder in man's relationship with God which only God could forgive. The teachers of the Law understood better than anyone else the ways in which God dealt with his people. Thus, when Jesus dared to speak the words "your sins are forgiven," they recognized immediately that something out of the ordinary had happened. These teachers then jumped to the conclusion that Jesus had usurped the prerogatives of God, failing to consider the possibility that God was doing something totally new in the history of his people. They were unable to see anything that did not accord with their pre-conceived notions of the way things have to be. They accused Jesus of blasphemy, i.e., demeaning God by assuming that a mere man could do what, in their view, only God could do.

This pronouncement story then reaches its climax with Jesus' statement:

> *The Son of Man has authority on earth to forgive sins (2:10).*

This statement is quite clear to us, the readers of Mark's Gospel. Jesus is claiming that he does indeed have the authority not only to cast out sickness and evil spirits but also to free man of the root cause of his alienation from God, namely sin. This meaning, however, would not have been at all clear to the contemporaries of Jesus. What does he mean by this strange expression, "Son of Man"? Is he speaking of himself or of someone else? These questions remain unanswered not only with the teachers of the Law but also with the disciples. Much later in the Gospel we shall see that even the disciples do not know what Jesus is talking about when he speaks of the Son of Man.

Here, however, the term "Son of Man" appears for the first time as part of Mark's deliberate plan gradually to unfold the reality of God's Kingdom. This term is used frequently in the second half of Mark's Gospel, but before the Caesarea Philippi incident (8:27) it appears only twice (2:10, 28). In neither of these two uses does Mark give any clear indication concerning what the term means or to whom it applies. A brief glance at some of its subsequent uses, however, will show that this term is rich in meaning concerning the reality of Jesus and the nature of the Good News of the Kingdom.

> *The Son of Man must suffer much and be rejected by the elders, the chief priests, and the teachers of the Law. He will be put to death, and after three days he will rise to life (8:31).*

> *If, then, a man is ashamed of me and of my teaching in this godless and wicked day, then the Son of Man will be ashamed of*

him when he comes in the glory of his Father with the holy
angels (8:38).

For even the Son of Man did not come to be served; he came to
serve and to give his life to redeem many people (10:45).

The Son of Man will die as the Scriptures say he will; but how
terrible for that man who will betray the Son of Man (14:21).

This fullness of meaning, however, is only dimly hinted at in
this story of the paralytic, the story with which Mark shows the
first indications of a conflict between the Good News and Judaism.

2. Only the Sick Need a Doctor, 2:13–17

The second pronouncement story of this section is introduced
by the call of another disciple, Levi, whom Matthew's Gospel
identifies as none other than the apostle Matthew himself. What
is significant for Mark, however, is that Levi is a tax collector.

The first group of disciples were likewise called from the shore
of Lake Galilee but they were fishermen. We know little about
them before their call but can assume that they were good Jews
and hard-working men whose occupation gave them symbolic
preparation for becoming fishers of men. Levi, on the other hand,
was not only not a good Jew but his occupation rendered him sin-
gularly ill-disposed for becoming a disciple of anyone.

In Jesus' day the Roman occupiers had a very effective method
for collecting taxes. They would sell to the inhabitants of the area
the right to collect taxes for them. These tax collectors, with the
authority of the Roman occupiers behind them, could then collect
from the people more than was just. They would pay the Romans
the original amount agreed upon and reap huge benefits for
themselves. It is little wonder that tax collectors were hated and
despised. They were excommunicated from the synagogue and
regarded as traitors to their own people.

In this section, so far, we have seen Jesus extend the healing
power of God's Kingdom to an outcast of society, forgive sins
and now call a man who is both an outcast and a sinner to be one

of his disciples. The pronouncement story which follows gives the reason for this unusual behavior:

> *People who are well do not need a doctor, but only those who are sick. I have not come to call the respectable people, but the outcasts (2:17).*

In this pronouncement story the scene is again set with persons hostile to Jesus, only here they are identified, for the first time, as Pharisees. In Jesus' time there were a variety of sects or parties within Judaism. In addition to the Pharisees the principal ones we meet in the Gospels are the Sadducees and the Herodians.

A century before Jesus there was a sharp division between those who supported the luxurious living and Hellenistic customs of the Hasmonean kings (the Sadducees) and those who adhered to a rigorous following of ancient Jewish customs and practices (the Pharisees). In the interim a new figure appeared on the scene, Herod the Great, appointed King of the Jews by the Romans. Herod was not a Jew by ancestry. He was an Idumean whose family had converted to Judaism during the Hasmonean expansion. In Jesus' day Herod's son, Antipas, was ruling in Galilee, but neither Antipas nor his father had ever really been accepted by the devout Pharisees or the aristocratic Sadducees. There had come to be, however, a group of supporters of Herod who saw in Herod and his family the best practical hope for sustaining the fortunes of the Jewish people.

There were teachers of the Law in all these sects or parties but the most rigorous and demanding of them were those of the Pharisees. The Pharisees have received a rather bad press in the New Testament because of their hostility to Jesus but in their own time they were regarded with high esteem, even by those who did not observe the rigorous pharisaic interpretation of the Law. Pharisees were like the few outstanding people that today live in each of our neighborhoods, i.e., good, holy people whom everyone admires but no one can quite imitate.

The new and perhaps startling insight provided by this story is that not even the best of people can live by their own efforts in God's Kingdom. Jesus' initial proclamation of the Good News in-

cluded a call to repentance and faith, i.e., a need to recognize that
there is something radically wrong with the way we are which
can be corrected only by staking our lives on Jesus. Not even the
best of people with their hair-splitting observance of the minuti-
ae of the Law could really live as God's children in his Kingdom.
If they could (or if anyone could) there would have been no need
for Jesus to live and die for us. Paul explains this insight in his
letter to the Galatians:

> *We know that a man is put right with God only through faith*
> *in Jesus Christ, never by doing what the Law requires. We, too,*
> *have believed in Christ Jesus in order to be put right with God*
> *through our faith in Christ, and not by doing what the Law*
> *requires. For no man is put right with God by doing what the*
> *Law requires (Gal 2:16).*

The scene for this pronouncement story, then, is set with re-
spectable people who feel they have made themselves right with
God by their observance of the Law. So jealous were they of their
standing with God that they would not jeopardize that standing
by touching a leper or by associating with sinners or traitors. So
comfortable were they with their own respectability that they
had no idea what Jesus was really up to.

The Good News of the Kingdom, however, is radically different from ordinary human ways of thinking about God, even the
very best. Jesus' pronouncement is probably intended as irony
and directed at those who think they can make themselves right
with God. Jesus' call extends to all mankind, for all are in need of
the healing power of God's Kingdom. The call is heard, however,
only by those who realize they are in need of healing and not by
those who think they have made themselves well.

3. Fasting in the Kingdom, 2:18–22

The role of repentance and the total newness of God's Kingdom are developed even further in this third pronouncement story which is based on a question about fasting. Fasting was
required by the Law of Moses on only one day of the year, Yom
Kippur, the Day of Atonement (Lv 16:29). On this day, a day set

aside for purification from sin, fasting was a sign of repentance, an act of self-deprivation by which one symbolized a readiness to turn away from one's former ways.

Both the followers of the Pharisees and the followers of John the Baptist fasted much more frequently than the Law required, while the disciples of Jesus did not. The Pharisees sought to make themselves right with God by an ever more perfect observance of the Law. They had built a hedge around the Law, hundreds of additional observances which would guarantee that the Law itself would be perfectly observed. By the time of Jesus it was customary for the Pharisees to fast on every Monday and Thursday.

The followers of John the Baptist fasted as well but for a different reason. John had taught that the time was about to come when God's salvation would finally be present among men. His followers fasted as a sign of repentance in preparation for this final moment of salvation.

The followers of Jesus, however, did not fast because in Jesus the moment of salvation had arrived. Jesus uses the image of the wedding party to explain this new situation. Just as everyone celebrates as long as the bridegroom is present, so also those who have turned away from their former way of life will continue to celebrate as long as the fullness of God's Kingdom is present to them in Jesus.

Verse 20 has caused problems for many commentators but can perhaps be explained as pointing to the mysterious already and not yet nature of God's Kingdom. The fullness of the Kingdom is already present in the person of Jesus. The Kingdom is already present in those who believe in Jesus but, at the same time, its perfect realization has not yet come. Because of the not yet aspect, repentance is not a once-for-all turning but rather an ongoing characteristic of Christian existence. Fasting as a Christian practice symbolizes this repentance precisely as it relates to the already and not yet nature of the Kingdom. The Lenten fast, for example, begins with the ashes of repentance and ends with the new light and life of Easter.

Verses 21 and 22, which were not part of the original pronouncement story, are sayings of Jesus added here because they develop additional aspects of the total newness of God's Kingdom. What the Law had prepared for has now arrived in the person and ministry of Jesus. The Pharisees had interpreted the Law, adapted it, built a hedge around it. They had tried to keep the Law current by patching it up over and over again. The Good News of the Kingdom, however, is not just another patch used to bring the Law up to date. The Good News of the Kingdom, as mentioned above, is not a matter of band-aids and aspirin; it is a radical new beginning.

Jesus was in no way a political or social revolutionary, but what happens in political and social revolutions can illustrate the meaning of these verses. In most revolutions, whether it be the French revolution or the Communist revolution in Russia or the recent Islamic revolution in Iran, there is an initial effort to accommodate the new ideas and energies within the old structures. If the revolution really strikes at the heart of the social or political system all such efforts will fail and a totally new structure will emerge. Jesus was proclaiming a totally new way of ordering man's relationship with God. There is no way in which this new reality could be accommodated within the confines of the Old Law any more than new wine could be poured into old wineskins. The Good News of the Kingdom of God has burst the boundaries and transcended the limitations of the Mosaic Law.

4. Lord of the Sabbath, 2:23–28

The seventh day of the week, a day of rest, a day consecrated to God is one of the most ancient observances in Israelite religion. With the Babylonian exile and the destruction of the temple the Sabbath acquired a new importance since most of the other religious practices were no longer possible. The Sabbath rest became the distinctive sign of God's chosen people.

> *I the Lord am your God; walk in my statutes, and be careful to observe my ordinances, and hallow my sabbaths that they may be a sign between me and you, that you may know that I the Lord am your God (Ez 20:19–20).*

The observance of the Sabbath became ever stricter as time went on. About two hundred years before Jesus a group of pious

Jews (predecessors of the Pharisees) allowed themselves to be slaughtered by the Seleucids rather than take up arms, even in self-defense, on the Sabbath (1 Mc 2:29–38). By the time of Jesus the Pharisees had a list of thirty-nine kinds of activity forbidden on the Sabbath, one of which was "reaping and threshing."

In this pronouncement story, then, the hostility of the Pharisees grows even more intense. In the previous story they complained because the disciples of Jesus did not fast. It was not a question of their violating the law of fast on the Day of Atonement but rather of not being as zealous as the Pharisees who fasted quite frequently. Here, however, the Pharisees complain because the disciples are blatantly violating one of the most sacred laws of Judaism by picking heads of wheat on the Sabbath.

Jesus responds to their criticism with three arguments which are progressively more difficult for the Pharisees to accept and which, in bringing out ever more clearly the true nature of the Good News, show the irreconcilability of God's Kingdom and pharisaic legalism.

a. The Law Can Be Disobeyed, 2:25–26

Jesus begins with an argument that even the Pharisees might accept. He cites an example from 1 Sm 21:2–7 in which David and his men clearly violated the Law. According to Lv 24:5–9 on each Sabbath bread was to be consecrated to the Lord which only the priests would be allowed to eat. David and his men were hungry one day and, since there was no other food available, the priest allowed them to eat the consecrated bread. Jesus' argument here rests on the fact that nowhere does God condemn David for his action, indicating that the intention of the Law itself is not as strict as the Pharisees maintain. This argument alone might have quieted the Pharisees, but Mark's purpose was not to appease the Pharisees but to proclaim the Good News. He thus proceeds to another of Jesus' arguments which the Pharisees were less likely to accept.

b. The Sabbath Was Made for Man, 2:27

This second argument focuses on the limited and imperfect nature of the Law itself. What is unlimited and perfect is the will of

God. The Law with all of its requirements was God's gift to his people and was intended to aid and guide them in living according to his will. The error of the Pharisees lay in their making the Law itself, including even their own additional requirements, the ultimate guiding principle.

It is not just the reordering of priorities which intensifies the hostility of the Pharisees. What really separates Jesus from the Pharisees is the suggestion, only hinted at here, that Jesus can make these statments because somehow he knows the ultimate will of God. This suggestion becomes explicit in the final argument which is the climactic statement of this pronouncement story.

c. The Son of Man Is Lord of the Sabbath, 2:28

Mark's procedure in leading up to this final statement with less weighty arguments is similar to the ploy of an Irish mayor in the last century. When ordered by a representative of Queen Victoria to have the bells of the town rung as the queen arrived for a visit, the mayor listed fifty reasons why he would not ring the bells. The last reason was that in his town there were no bells.

The Kingdom of God, a totally new reality above and beyond the Law, has arrived on the scene. The mysterious Son of Man mentioned in the first pronouncement story appears again in the last. The Son of Man can not only forgive sins but he is so intimate with the perfect will of God that even the Law is subject to him. The Sabbath law, then, has no binding force at all in the presence of the Son of Man, in the presence of this totally new reality which is God's Kingdom.

We, the readers of Mark's Gospel, know that Jesus is speaking of himself. The characters here portrayed by Mark, however, do not. They only perceive that Jesus, by his actions and explanations, is claiming the presence of a new way of life which rejects and supersedes pharisaic legalism. Whoever Jesus is, he is a threat to the established way of life in first-century Judaism.

C. REJECTION BY JUDAISM, 3:1–6

OVERVIEW. The story about the man with the crippled hand brings to a conclusion the series of conflict stories in this section of Mark's Gospel. Like the first story in that series, the story about the paralytic, this story combines features of a miracle story and a pronouncement story. Here too Jesus' pronouncement is more important than the miracle he performs, but what is most significant in this story is the final observation that the Pharisees and Herodians are planning to kill Jesus.

1. In the Synagogue on a Sabbath, 3:1–2

The synagogue, like the Sabbath, achieved its prominence in Jewish life as a result of the Babylonian exile and the destruction of the temple. Even after the second temple was built the synagogue remained as a center for the study of the Law. In Jesus' time the synagogues of Galilee, because of the distance from Jerusalem, were the focus for both study and worship. In the first section of Mark's Gospel Jesus is often in the synagogue preaching and healing (1:21, 23, 29, 39). In the second section (1:40—3:6) he returns to the synagogue only once (3:1) to speak his final word and work his last miracle before his rejection by Judaism. We will see him in the synagogue only once more, at the end of the next section (6:1), when he returns to Nazareth only to be rejected by the people of his home town.

The Sabbath and the synagogue are clearly connected by Mark, for apart from the incident in Nazareth, which also happens on a Sabbath, Mark records no further activity of Jesus on that day of the week. The first section of Mark's Gospel (1:14–39) showed Jesus proclaiming the Good News in the context of Judaism. The second section (1:41—3:6) shows how the Good News of the Kingdom, as its nature became clearer, is irreconcilably opposed to the Judaism practiced in Jesus' day.

2. To Save Or To Destroy, 3:3–4

For the Pharisees, every sort of work was forbidden on the Sabbath, even the work of a physician. Only in cases of life or death was anyone permitted to heal on the Sabbath. Here we see

Jesus not only on the Sabbath but also in a synagogue confronted by a man with a crippled hand, hardly a case of life or death. Those who had grown suspicious of Jesus were waiting to see if he was really so disdainful of the Law that he would violate the Sabbath even in a synagogue.

Jesus, however, was doing something to which their eyes and hearts were blind, i.e., bringing in God's Kingdom. He said to the man, "Come up here to the front" (3:3). Here, as in the story of Simon's mother-in-law, Mark uses the same Greek verb he will use to describe Jesus' resurrection (14:28; 16:6). What Jesus is doing for people is not just curing illnesses but helping people to enter the new life of God's Kingdom. Jesus' question, then, is rich with this added meaning.

> *What does our Law allow us to do on the Sabbath? To help or to harm? To save a man's life, or to destroy it? (3:4).*

The alternatives are clear. To refuse to help a person is actually to harm him. To refuse to save a man's life is actually to destroy it. Jesus, true to his mission to bring God's Kingdom to all men, really has no choice. He welcomes the man with the crippled hand into God's Kingdom.

3. Silence and Anger, 3:4–5

This story about the man with the crippled hand is seen by Mark as a foretaste of Jesus' teaching on the Great Commandment of Love. At the end of the passage on the Love Command we read:

> *After this nobody dared to ask Jesus any more questions (12:34).*

Their silence there, as here, is an indication not of agreement or acceptance but of obstinacy and rejection. There in the temple in Jerusalem they are about to finalize their plans to eliminate this strange man. Here, in a synagogue in Galilee, the decision is first made that the irreconcilable opposition between Jesus and Judaism requires that he be done away with.

Jesus is aware of the meaning of their silence. He is angry.

When he saw the leper at the beginning of this section he was filled with pity (1:41). He saw a need for the healing power of God's Kingdom and was moved to satisfy that need. Now, in a similar situation, he sees a refusal to accept the healing power of God's Kingdom, a refusal based on the conviction that everything is fine just the way it is. Jesus' opponents were like astronomers of a few centuries ago, satisfied with their conviction that the earth was the center of the universe and refusing to consider any other possibility.

4. Rejection and Death, 3:6

The first section of Mark's Gospel (1:14–39) showed Jesus casting out demons and curing illness. Its focus was the new life of God's Kingdom. It concluded with a veiled allusion to Jesus' resurrection (1:35–39). This section (1:40—3:6) delves further into the meaning of the Good News, showing Jesus exercising authority over sin, an authority which is superior to the Law. It concludes here with an explicit reference to his death (3:6).

"Strange bedfellows" is a phrase used in the modern political scene to describe a rather unusual situation when customary opponents join forces. When a matter appears before Congress supported by both a liberal Democrat and a conservative Republican we can be certain that something extraordinary is happening. When the devout Pharisees and the opportunistic Herodians join forces to overcome a threat, it is no ordinary threat that they are dealing with. What Jesus is proclaiming is so radically new that it transcends all current political and religious differences.

Mark has only begun to tell his story and already the death of Jesus is decided upon. Here, however, his death is presented simply as the result of opposition from parties hostile to the Good News. In the second half of the Gospel (8:27—16:8), as Mark continues to unfold the full reality of God's Kingdom, he will show how suffering and death are not just the result of opposition but are essential aspects of the Good News itself.

STUDY QUESTIONS

1. Jesus touched the leper (1:41). Are there people today we are unwilling to touch? Have we been touched by Jesus? Are we as eager as the leper to spread the Good News?

2. Why do we sin (2:5)? Do we enjoy being proud, cruel or selfish? Can Jesus take away the root cause of the disorders that affect our lives?

3. Who were the Pharisees? Were they good people? How were they regarded by the Jews of their day? What was the basic opposition between Jesus and the Pharisees?

4. Who were the Herodians? Why were they afraid of Jesus? Why did the Pharisees join them in plotting Jesus' death (3:6)? To what extent are we, like the Pharisees and Herodians, afraid of Jesus?

5. What kind of a revolutionary was Jesus? In what did his revolution consist? Why did he permit the picking of wheat on the Sabbath (2:23)?

Chapter Three

THE NEW PEOPLE OF GOD

SUMMARY. Salvation was first offered to the chosen people of the Old Testament but they rejected the offer. In this chapter we will see Jesus choosing a new people of God and explaining, by words and deeds, the Good News of salvation.

Twelve apostles are chosen as symbols of the twelve tribes of Israel, but membership in God's people no longer depends on blood relationships. Not even blood relationship with Jesus matters in the Kingdom of God. What God's Kingdom really consists in, however, remains a mystery, a mystery that cannot be explained in ordinary human language.

We will consider, therefore, the unusual kinds of words and deeds by which Jesus explains the unexplainable, i.e., his parabolic words and deeds, especially his parables and miracles.

As the mystery of the Kingdom of God begins to unfold we can share with Jesus' followers the enormous difficulty of understanding the Good News. We can perhaps even appreciate the attitude of the people of Nazareth who could not go beyond surface appearances. We can ask ourselves whether we today go beyond surface appearances.

READ 3:7–6:6

OVERVIEW. In this section Mark continues to tell the story of the Good News by showing Jesus' mission both broadening and narrowing. Jesus, here, will proclaim the Good News in both word and deed beyond the borders of Jewish territory. He will explain how membership in God's family is in no way restricted. At the same time, however, Jesus continues to experience misunderstanding and rejection. Even more, he deliberately restricts his clearest teaching to the narrow band of twelve.

The first section (1:14–39) opened as this section does with a summary statement of Jesus' preaching followed by a call to discipleship (compare 1:14–20 with 3:7–19). The first section continued with Jesus entering a synagogue and teaching (1:21). This section, however, will end with Jesus teaching in a synagogue for the last time in Mark's Gospel (6:1–6). What Mark is doing in this section is shifting his focus away from the Jews and onto the new people of God constituted by the Good News of the Kingdom.

A. NEW BEGINNING, 3:7–19

1. Summary, 3:7–12

This section opens with a scene in which Jesus is again proclaiming the Good News before a crowd assembled at the shores of Lake Galilee. The Pharisees and Herodians were plotting to kill Jesus but he still enjoyed immense popularity with the people. What is unusual about this crowd is that they have come not only from Galilee but from other areas inhabited by Jews (Judea, Jerusalem, Idumea) as well as from two neighboring Gentile areas (on the east: the other side of the Jordan; and on the north: Tyre and Sidon). The people coming from Jewish areas serve as a prelude to the opponents of Jesus who appear in 3:22. The people from Gentile areas prepare us for Jesus' eventual ministry in both of these regions (see 5:1; 7:24, 31).

The large crowd that comes to see Jesus comes because "they heard of the things he was doing" (3:8). There is no indication that they understood what he was doing beyond a superficial awareness of miracle-working. They had heard that his miraculous cures resulted from touch (see 1:41), so they tried to benefit from his miraculous power by touching him. We will consider

the truth and the error in this view when we discuss the story of the woman with severe bleeding (5:25–34).

Although the people have only a limited appreciation of who Jesus is and what he is really doing, the demons are fully aware. Whenever they see him they address him by his correct title, "Son of God" (3:11; see also 5:7). The demons call Jesus by his correct title because, in the Semitic mentality, to be able to name something was to exercise control over it (see the story of Adam naming the creatures, Gn 2:19–20). Thus both in the summary and in the story of the man with evil spirits (5:1–20) we see futile efforts on the part of demons to control or neutralize the power of Jesus.

The demons' efforts to control Jesus fail but mention of this event here serves two purposes for Mark. First, the absolute superiority and inviolability of the Kingdom of God is restated. Second, with Jesus' command that the evil spirits be silent (3:12), the paradox which will dominate the rest of this section is established. The Kingdom of God is absolute, extending its power everywhere; at the same time, however, it is concealed so that very few catch even a glimpse of it.

2. Appointment of the Twelve, 3:13–19

Immediately after showing a huge crowd from different lands coming to Jesus to experience the reality of God's Kingdom, Mark moves in the opposite direction. Here he shows Jesus narrowing down the number to be with him, to share with him his life in God's Kingdom. The number Jesus selects is twelve, a number which signifies fullness or completion. This number appears in the Old Testament as the number of Jacob's sons (Gn 35:22–26), the heads of the twelve tribes of Israel. What Jesus is doing is starting all over again, forming a new people of God which will begin with the twelve apostles.

The crucial importance of this passage for Mark can be seen by comparing it with the corresponding passage in Matthew's Gospel.

Mt 10:1–2	Mk 3:13–16
Jesus called his twelve disciples together and gave them authority to drive out the evil spirits and every sickness. These are the names of the twelve apostles. . . .	Then Jesus *went up a hill* and called to himself the men he wanted. *They came to him* and he chose twelve, whom he named apostles. *"I have chosen you to be with me,"* he told them; "I will also send you out to preach, and you will have authority to drive out demons." These are the twelve he chose. . . .

The italicized phrases, which do not appear in Matthew, are all very significant for Mark. The hill is a place where solemn acts occur, a place of revelation like Mount Sinai where God gave his Law to Moses and constituted the Hebrew people as his special people. A similar setting does appear in Matthew's Gospel:

> *Jesus saw the crowds and went up a hill, where he sat down. His disciples gathered around him, and he began to teach them. . . .*
> *(Mt 5:1–2).*

Since Matthew tells his story from the perspective of Jesus' teaching, the solemn, revelatory act in the first part of his Gospel is the Sermon on the Mount.

This sermon is seen by Matthew as fulfilling the Law given on Mount Sinai. For Mark, however, it is the appointment of the twelve, as the beginning of the new people of God, that signals the end of the Law of Moses and the beginning of the Good News of salvation. From this point onward "the twelve" are the dominant figures in Mark's Gospel. The perspective from which Mark tells his story is not Jesus' teaching or even his deeds but rather how the twelve disciples respond to what Jesus says and does.

Mark, in this account, emphasized the disciples' coming to Jesus and Jesus' choosing them to be with him. The expressions "with me," "with him," and "with Jesus" occur repeatedly throughout Mark's Gospel as the characteristic expression for that intimate relationship which is Christian discipleship. Mark tells his story of the Good News from the perspective of the twelve living their discipleship, being "with Jesus." A critical moment, then, will be reached in Mark's Gospel when this intimacy is shattered—when Judas is with a crowd (14:43) and Peter is "with the guards" (14:54).

B. EXTENT OF GOD'S KINGDOM, 3:20–35

OVERVIEW. Jesus, while proclaiming the Good News to an even larger and more diverse audience, begins to limit his intimate communication of God's Kingdom. Why? Who really belongs to God's Kingdom? In what does membership in God's family consist?

In this passage Mark begins to consider these questions by showing how different groups of people respond to Jesus' proclamation of the Good News. Mark, throughout his Gospel, will show various degrees of praise, sympathy or condemnation for the diverse reactions to Jesus' proclamation. In this passage Mark will express this diversity using a device known as intercalation, i.e., inserting one incident between two sections of another incident: the Beelzebul incident (3:22–30) is inserted between two sections of the family incident (3:20–21, 31–35). This same device shows up in four other places in Mark's Gospel (5:21–43; 6:7–30; 11:12–26; 14:1–11).

1. Beelzebul, 3:22–30

Just as Galilee has symbolic meaning in Mark's Gospel, so too does Jerusalem. Three times people from Jerusalem come to Jesus: first, just to see this marvelous person in operation (3:8); second, in our present passage, to accuse him of demonic possession (3:22); and finally, in the next section, to accuse him of departing from the teachings of their ancestors (7:1). Jerusalem will not be mentioned again until the third and final passion prediction (10:32) after which Jesus will enter Jerusalem three times on three successive days as a prelude to his death (11:11, 15, 27). We will explore the symbolism of "three" later on in our study; here it is Jerusalem that is significant.

Jesus had been teaching with authority. He had been working miracles. News about him had spread to Jerusalem and beyond. People were amazed at his power and authority and they wondered about who he was and what the source of his power might be. The teachers of the Law in Jerusalem, the true center of Judaism, saw him as a threat and felt it was their duty to expose him before the people as an agent of Satan.

Actually the teachers of the Law made two separate accusations, the second more serious than the first. Prior to the insertion of this incident Jesus' family had accused him of being insane (3:21). Now the teachers of the Law maintain that it is not insanity but demonic possession that accounts for his strange behavior. He is possessed, they say, by a demon named Beelzebul. Some among them go a step further and level an even more serious charge. Jesus was not just behaving strangely as would one who was insane or possessed. Jesus was behaving so powerfully that he actually must have formed an alliance with Satan himself.

Jesus does not respond to these accusations by explaining that he is in fact the Son of God who came to inaugurate the Kingdom of God. Instead he responds with two parabolic utterances (see 3:23). This is the first time in Mark where the hidden quality of Jesus' teaching is explicitly indicated, though up to this point everything Jesus said and did was veiled and hidden. Why, however, does Jesus not explain plainly and openly who he is and what the Kingdom of God is all about?

PARABOLIC TEACHING

The realization of the Kingdom of God in our lives depends most essentially on faith, on a personal relationship of trust with Jesus. The communication of what is involved in the Kingdom depends as well on this personal relationship. Jesus' parabolic language, then, is somewhat like the language spoken by a man and a woman in love. Lovers usually acquire a vocabulary of words, phrases, and images that only they understand, a vocabulary that apart from their relationship of love is meaningless, but a vocabulary that in the context of their relationship communicates far more richly and abundantly than any kind of direct speech could. The reality of God's Kingdom cannot be encompassed by direct, logical language. It can only be expressed in open-ended, parabolic words and deeds. It can only be understood by those who have already entered into a personal relationship with Jesus.

Jesus responds, then, to the charges of the teachers of the Law with two parables, parables which he addresses not to the teachers of the Law but to the people who have some beginnings of faith in him (3:23). The first parable is quite clear in its meaning as we read it today (3:24–27).

Jesus could not be possessed, for demons do not fight against demons. Jesus could not be an agent of Satan, for he is actually stronger than Satan and is presently overpowering him. Our understanding, however, flows from hindsight. For the hearers of Jesus' day this parable was open-ended and left many questions unanswered, questions which the teachers of the Law would probably have answered incorrectly.

The second parable (3:28–29) focuses on the most serious aspect of the accusation against Jesus. Since everything Jesus does he does by the Spirit of God, to attribute his actions to Satan is to speak evil of the Spirit of God, i.e., to blaspheme. Jesus' response is actually the most solemn pronouncement we have encountered thus far in Mark's Gospel.

> *Remember this! Men can be forgiven all their sins and all the evil things they may say. But whoever says evil things against the Holy Spirit will never be forgiven (3:28–29).*

The phrase which our version translates here as "remember this" and elsewhere as "I tell you this" is really a much more powerful expression. Many versions translate it as:

> *"Amen, I say to you."*

The word "Amen" is a Semitic word which involves the faith relationship of taking one's stand on another person. The Jews of Jesus' day used the word to affirm or approve the words of another. They used the word very much in the way we now use it in prayer. However, our use of it as a formal response to a prayer (. . . forever and ever, Amen) is often less expressive of its real meaning than is the enthusiastic response of a congregation to a preacher giving eloquent expression to their common faith (. . . Amen, brother).

Usually people (in Jesus' day as in our own) used the word to indicate their willingness to take their stand on what had been said. Jesus, however, uses "Amen" to introduce his own words, his most solemn affirmations. By his use of this word he is saying:

> *You can stake your life on my words.*

He is saying, in effect, that his words are reliable and true with a truth and a reliability one could expect from God alone. Mark shows Jesus using this solemn kind of affirmation thirteen times in his Gospel but only twice in the first half (3:28; 8:12).

With this first use of the expression an important distinction is made between a failure to see the Good News of the Kingdom in Jesus' miracles and a refusal to see. The crowds who think that

Jesus is a miracle-worker or even his family who think he is insane can easily be forgiven. Their failure is the result of understandable human weakness. The attribution of Jesus' power to Satan, however, is blasphemy against the spirit. Its unforgivableness comes from the fact that it consists in defiant resistance and is not just a failure to recognize the work of the Spirit in Jesus.

2. True Family of Jesus, 3:20–21, 31–35

Framing this incident on defiant resistance is the less serious but more instructive incident about the failure of Jesus' own family to see beyond surface appearances. What they see is a relative of theirs who has become so totally involved with the crowds chasing after him that he no longer takes care of himself. We are twice told that he does not even have time to eat (3:20; 6:31) and may presume that he has become negligent regarding other basic needs as well. What his relatives can see with their eyes causes such great anxiety that they are incapable of seeing the real significance of Jesus' behavior. His family arrives at the understandable and forgivable conclusion:

He's gone mad! (3:21).

What is really instructive about this incident, however, is what appears in the second part (3:31–35). There we are given a picture of the new people of God, Mark's main concern in this third section of his Gospel. Jesus is inside the house surrounded by a crowd which included both the twelve and other followers. What is significant is that they are inside with Jesus while his blood relatives are outside. By this arrangement of the characters Mark has symbolized what he has been teaching all along, i.e., living in God's Kingdom involves being with Jesus. Here, however, Mark carries his unfolding of the reality of God's Kingdom one dramatic step further.

Living in God's Kingdom involves not only being with Jesus but also being, in a real sense, members of his family. What this ultimately implies is that if Jesus is God's Son, then those with him are God's children. Since Mark is still concealing Jesus' identity as God's Son he does not draw out this implication. He does, however, provide us with one additional insight into the reality of God's Kingdom.

> *Whoever does what God wants him to do is my brother, my sister, my mother (3:35).*

The Good News of salvation is that the time has arrived when it is possible to do the will of God. We have known this fact from the very beginning but in the unfolding process of Mark's Gospel it has remained hidden up to now. Here, as Mark paints a picture of the new people of God, he clearly shows that membership in this new people not only involves being part of Jesus' family but also that it has nothing to do with blood or ethnic relationship. The sole determining factor is doing the will of God.

Mark is concerned about the will of God throughout his Gospel but rarely mentions it. In fact there is only one other place in the entire Gospel where he speaks of God's will, the only place where he shows someone perfectly fulfilling God's will. In the garden of Gethsemane Jesus prays:

> *My Father! All things are possible for you. Take this cup away from me. But not what I want, but what you want (14:36).*

These two passages (3:35 and 14:36) by their appearance at critical junctures in Mark's Gospel are most instructive in showing what membership in the new people of God really involves. It involves being with Jesus and like Jesus in perfect openness to God's will whatever that will might involve.

C. THE HIDDEN KINGDOM, 4:1—5:43

OVERVIEW. The Kingdom of God can only be seen by one who has faith. Its mysterious and transcendent nature is such that it can only be proclaimed in a hidden and veiled manner. Those who have faith will see through the veil according to the degree of their faith. In this way their faith will gradually increase as will their appreciation of and incorporation into the Kingdom of God.

In Mk 4 and 5 Jesus continues to proclaim the Good News of the Kingdom by word and deed. Although the Kingdom remains hidden Jesus becomes explicit about its hidden character. Here, however, we begin to see the twelve, the most favored of his hearers, failing to penetrate the veil. We will first see Jesus proclaiming the Kingdom in parables, words which point beyond themselves to an inexpressible reality, and then in miracles, deeds which point beyond themselves to the same inexpressible reality.

In 3:23 Mark introduced for the first time the idea of parabolic utterances. Here Mark explains what parabolic teaching is by giving several instructive examples. The term "parable" can have both a broad and a narrow meaning. Any kind of figurative speech can be called a parable in the broad sense. In its most narrow sense, however, a parable is a type of a simile, namely, a simile which is expanded into a story.

In an ordinary simile there is a single image used for comparison, used to give figurative expression to an idea, e.g., "he fought like a lion." When Jesus expands the single image into a story we have a parable in the strictest sense, e.g.,

> *The Kingdom of God is like a man who scatters seed in his field.*
> *He sleeps at night. . . . (4:26–29).*

Here, as in the ordinary simile, there is a single comparison made. The Kingdom of God is not like a man or like a seed or like a field; it is like the whole situation described in the story. Parables, then, are very different from allegories where every element in the story corresponds to something. The function of the parable is to paint a picture that will lead the mind to that single point of comparison. C.H. Dodd has given us an excellent definition of a parable:

> *A metaphor or simile drawn from nature or common life,*
> *arresting the hearer by its vividness or strangeness, and leaving*
> *the mind in sufficient doubt about its precise application to tease it*
> *into active thought (*The Parables of the Kingdom, N.Y.,
> 1961, p. 5).

All of the different kinds of parables which Jesus used function in precisely the way Dodd described. They are designed to involve the hearer in the situation, trouble the hearer by the strangeness of the situation, and challenge the hearer to go beyond the situation to an appreciation of what the Kingdom of God is all about.

Parables, then, function just like miracles since both are veiled forms of proclaiming the Good News of the Kingdom. Both are forms of proclamation that cannot be received passively but rather demand some kind of personal involvement and commitment. We shall see, as we examine the parables and miracles that follow, that many failed to make this personal commitment and remained in the dark concerning the reality of God's Kingdom.

1. Parables, 4:1–34

a. The Sower, 4:1–9

In this and the following passages we have a mixture of teachings in parables and teachings about parables. This first passage (4:1–9) is both; it has often been described as a parable about parables. The verse introducing the parable of the sower is instructive:

> *He used parables to teach them many things, and in his teaching*
> *he said to them. . . . (4:2).*

Though Mark tells us that Jesus taught many things in parables, he actually includes very few of them in his Gospel. Some of the most familiar of Jesus' parables, e.g., the Good Samaritan, the Pharisee and the Publican, etc., are to be found in Matthew and Luke but not in Mark. Mark is more interested in showing how Jesus taught and how various groups of people reacted to his teaching than he is in detailing the actual content of Jesus' teaching. What follows, then, is a parable about the way Jesus taught about the Kingdom of God.

The parable is introduced and concluded by the same warning:

Listen (4:3).

Listen, then, if you have ears to hear with (4:9).

There is more to this story than lies on the surface, but many will fail to go beyond what first meets the ears.

This story, like all the parables, is a somewhat true to life story that would have sounded very familiar to the audience of Jesus. They are only somewhat true to life because there is usually some aspect of the story that does not quite fit. It is this strange or unusually vivid aspect that teases and challenges the mind to go beyond surface appearances. Everything in this story about the sower is quite ordinary, even the birds and the thorns. What is unusual is the harvest. A twenty-fold harvest would have been extraordinary. What Jesus suggests here is a thirty- or sixty- or even hundred-fold harvest. Do we hear what Jesus is saying? (If not, then let us read on!)

b. Purpose of Parables, 4:10–12

Jesus did not teach in parables to prevent people from understanding him. He taught in parables because they were the only form of speech capable of expressing a reality beyond the possibility of ordinary human expression. The result of his teaching in parables, however, was an ever clearer division between those "with Jesus" and those who chose to remain "outside" (4:11), between those who took their stand on Jesus and accepted his challenge to strain beyond appearances and those who stood on their own ground and refused to budge.

The secret of the Kingdom of God, given to those with Jesus, is simply this ability to see beyond appearances, to see in the parables and miracles of Jesus the reality of God's Kingdom. The word of God first spoken by the prophet Isaiah (Is 6:9–10) is fulfilled again and again whenever people choose to set their own standards and provide for their own security:

> *They may look and look, yet not see,*
> *they may listen and listen, yet not understand;*

for if they did, they would turn to God
and he would forgive them (4:12).

c. Explanation of the Parable of the Sower, 4:13–20

In a recent contest a prize was to be given for the most difficult to answer question. The winner was the person who submitted the question: "Why can't we tickle ourselves?" We simply cannot, but we probably cannot explain why. Parables share something of the mystery of a tickle, and the fact of the matter is that they cannot be explained. If they could be explained there would have been no need for Jesus to speak in parables in the first place.

We do, however, try to explain parables. We actually have in Mk 4:13–20 an explanation of a parable. All explanations, however, are inadequate. If someone tells a funny story, a joke, everyone laughs spontaneously except those who failed to grasp the punch line. We can then explain the punch line to them but they probably will not laugh, at least not spontaneously. A joke that has to be explained loses its power to generate laughter. A parable that has to be explained loses its power to tease us beyond the surface toward a fuller appreciation of the Kingdom of God.

When Jesus has to explain the parable of the sower to the disciples, Mark is, for the first time, presenting the disciples as those who have been called, who are with Jesus, who have received the ability to see beyond and yet who fail to see the full reality of God's Kingdom. Their lack of understanding becomes the chief focus of the next section of Mark's Gospel (6:6—8:26). Here, however, it is presented to dramatize the importance of understanding Jesus' veiled manner of teaching. The question asked by Jesus in 4:13 could be rephrased:

If you cannot understand the parable about parables, how will
you ever understand any parable?

The explanation that follows is not so much an explanation of the parable but an explanation, using details from the parable, of why people fail to understand parables. All of the explanations are sympathetic and could easily fit the disciples or those of Mark's readers whom he intends to instruct by means of the dis-

ciples. It is significant that Jesus makes no mention of those outside, of those who refuse to listen. His concern here is entirely
with those who do listen but who, in the not yet time of salvation, are torn by rival Kingdoms.

The final line of the explanation comes closest to being an explanation of the parable itself. The Kingdom of God is a hidden
Kingdom. It has already arrived in the person of Jesus. It is already being made available to everyone, but its fullness is not
yet. What we have already is hidden and veiled. What we have
already is threatened by powers that might seem overwhelming.
What we have already, however, will ultimately triumph with a
success beyond our wildest imagination. All of the parables of Jesus, these hidden and veiled manifestations of the Kingdom,
point to the fullness of that Kingdom, a reality which neither our
minds nor our words can comprehend.

d. The Lamp and the Rule, 4:21–25

The two parables in this passage are parables in the broad
sense, figurative expressions which point to a reality beyond
themselves. Mark inserts them here because they develop the two
main ideas of the sower parable, the hidden quality of the Kingdom and the necessity to see the Kingdom even though it is hidden.

Jesus does not teach in parables, as we said above, to conceal
the Good News. His purpose in coming into the world was to
bring the Good News of the Kingdom to all. He proclaims the
Good News in the only way possible, in parables and miracles,
but with the clear intent that it be heard and seen.

> *Whatever is hidden away will be brought out into the open, and
> whatever is covered up will be uncovered (4:22).*

The Good News of the Kingdom is like a lamp set on a stand
for all to see, but the fact of the matter is that it is not seen by all.
The fault, however, is not with Jesus' proclamation of the Kingdom (even though it is hidden) but with the response of those
who judge by their own standards and refuse to have faith in Jesus.

The same rules you use to judge others will be used by God to judge you (4:24).

If we choose to take our stand on anything other than Jesus we blind ourselves to the reality of the Good News and have only ourselves to blame. If, on the other hand, we take our stand on Jesus no matter how weak and hesitant our faith may be, the full reality of God's Kingdom will be unfolded for us.

The man who has something will be given more (4:25).

Only the person who refuses to look beyond himself, who blasphemes against the Holy Spirit when the hidden reality of the Kingdom is present to him, will suffer eternal deprivation.

The man who has nothing will have taken away from him the little he has (4:25).

e. The Seed and the Mustard Seed, 4:26–34

This final passage on parables includes two short parables, both of which, like the parable of the sower (4:3–9), deal with seeds and growth. All three of these parables were vehicles that Jesus used to tease people into an appreciation of the already and not yet nature of God's Kingdom. Each of them, however, has its own special focus.

The parable of the sower focused on the extraordinary outcome that is achieved in spite of the thoroughly understandable obstacles that lie in its way. In the parable of the growing seed (4:26–29) no mention is made of obstacles; instead, attention is focused on the power present in the seed itself. There is a shift in emphasis from the not yet of the Kingdom to the already of the Kingdom. The Kingdom of God in which we already live, though it is quiet and often barely perceptible, is real and powerful. Though Christians live in constant expectation of the end time, the period between sowing and harvesting is not insignificant. The natural and necessary process of growth and maturation is as much a part of the Kingdom of God as is its arrival and its completion.

The final parable, the parable of the mustard seed (4:30–32), shifts the emphasis again. Here there is no mention of a harvest but only of the contrast between what we now have and what we began with. This parable completes the process which Mark follows, here as elsewhere, of moving from a general proclamation of the Good News to a more intimate instruction for the disciples. The last parable applies most specifically to the disciples as the model community of faith. The lesson of this parable could be paraphrased and addressed to any Christian community:

> *If you have any doubts about the power of God's Kingdom just look at yourselves. Your community which began as a simple response of faith is now a center of growth, encouragement, support and protection for yourselves and all who join you.*

Of course this paraphrase is not, in any sense, an adequate explanation of the parable. Parables cannot be explained. They can only be allowed to tease and to point beyond themselves to an inexpressible reality. Parables are meant to challenge us to decide for or against this new reality. Parables were also an effective tool which Jesus used to proclaim the Kingdom in measured doses. The full reality of the Good News would have been too much for anyone to accept all at once. Paul was speaking about this same difficulty when he wrote:

> *I could not talk to you as I talk to men who have the Spirit; I had to talk to you as men of this world, as children in the Christian faith. I had to feed you milk, not solid food, because you were not ready for it (1 Cor 3:1–2).*

As Mark expresses it, Jesus taught in parables in order to teach "as much as they could understand" (4:33). The disciples, however, were capable of more than the crowds. They were "with Jesus." Their personal relationship with Jesus enabled them to grasp more fully the reality of the Kingdom. Mark's assertion that "he would explain everything to them" (4:34) is, however, clearly an overstatement. As we shall soon see, the disciples, to whom the most has been revealed, will be the most severely chastised for their failure to understand.

2. Miracles, 4:35–5:43

OVERVIEW. After using parables to teach about the Kingdom of God and specifically about its hidden quality, Mark returns to having Jesus proclaim the Good News of the Kingdom in miracles. Now, however, it should be clear to us, the readers, that miracles like parables are a form of veiled proclamation. After telling us that the twelve had been set apart for special instruction (4:34), Mark begins with a story about a miracle which demonstrates the disciples' lack of faith (4:40). This series of miracle stories will end with Jesus allowing only three, Peter, James, and John, to witness his most extraordinary feat (5:36). These same three will be with Jesus on the mountain of the transfiguration (9:2) and will fail him in the garden of Gethsemane (14:33–41).

a. Jesus Calms a Storm, 4:35–41

Most of the miracles in Mark's Gospel involve casting out demons or some kind of infirmity, i.e., freeing people from the power of Satan and welcoming them into the Kingdom of God. Here, however, we have the first example of a nature miracle, a miracle in which Jesus alters the natural state of things around him.

Healing miracles are proclamations in deed of the Good News of the Kingdom. Nature miracles proclaim the same Good News but are actually more like parables than are healing miracles. First, the evil that is overcome is not a real effect of the Kingdom of Satan but a symbolic effect, e.g., the behavior of a storm at sea, raging and doing violence, is very much like the behavior of a man possessed by an evil spirit. Second, while healing miracles are performed for the benefit of the one healed and are often done in secret, nature miracles are performed for the benefit of those who see them. Like parables, the action performed teases the mind and challenges the person who sees it to accept the full reality of the Kingdom toward which the miracle points.

In this miracle story we see Jesus speaking to the winds and

waves in the same way he spoke to the evil spirit in the very first
miracle of Mark's Gospel:

> *Jesus commanded the spirit, "Be quiet, and come out of the man!"*
> *(1:25).*

> *Jesus got up and commanded the wind, "Be quiet!" and said to*
> *the waves, "Be still!" (4:39).*

We also see in this miracle story an aspect of the Kingdom of God
parabolically portrayed. The Kingdom already is like a mustard
tree but it is not yet free from the threats of the Kingdom of Satan. In the Kingdom of God, however, we may be confident that,
having taken our stand on Jesus, he is with us and will protect us.
In John's Gospel Jesus says:

> *I have told you this so that you will have peace by being united*
> *to me. The world will make you suffer. But be brave! I have*
> *defeated the world! (Jn 16:33).*

The disciples, however, have not learned the lessons of the parables. They are not brave. Jesus rebukes them for their lack of
faith.

> *Why are you frightened? Are you still without faith? (4:40).*

The disciples, in failing to understand the parables, fail to trust in
Jesus in time of peril. They still do not understand who Jesus is
(4:41). Even less do they understand the real meaning of the Good
News he is proclaiming.

b. The Gerasene Demoniac, 5:1–20

The other side of Lake Galilee where this miracle took place
was a predominantly Gentile area often referred to as the Decapolis, the region of ten Greek cities. Rejected by the leaders of
the Jews and not understood by even his own disciples, Jesus
turns for the first time to a Gentile area.

This miracle story, as we mentioned in chapter one, is an excellent example of the kind of eyewitness detail to be found in Mark's Gospel. If we compare the corresponding accounts of Matthew and Mark we see, first, that they agree on the main substance of what happened; second, that Matthew has altered some aspects of the story; and, finally, that Mark preserves an abundance of precise detail that is best explained by assuming his version is very close to an eyewitness account.

Mt 8:28–34	Mk 5:1–17
[28] Jesus came to the territory of the Gadarenes, on the other side of the lake, and was met by two men who came out of the burial caves. These men had demons in them and were so fierce that no one dared travel on that road.	[1] They arrived on the other side of Lake Galilee, at the territory of the Gerasenes. [2] As soon as Jesus got out of the boat he was met by a man who came out of the burial caves. [3] This man had an evil spirit in him and lived among the graves. Nobody could keep him tied with chains any more; [4] many times his feet and hands had been tied, but every time he broke the chains, and smashed the irons on his feet. He was too strong for anyone to stop him. [5] Day and night he wandered among the graves and through the hills, screaming and cutting himself with stones.
[29] At once they screamed, "What do you want with us, Son of God? Have you come to punish us before the right time?"	[6] He was some distance away when he saw Jesus; so he ran, fell on his knees before him, [7] and screamed in a loud voice, "Jesus, Son of the Most High God! What do you want with me!" [8] (He said this because Jesus was saying to him, "Evil spirit, come out of this man!") [9] So Jesus asked him, "What is your name?" The man answered, "My name is 'Mob'—there are so many of us!" [10] And he kept begging Jesus not to send the evil spirits out of that territory.
[30] Not far away a large herd of pigs was feeding.	[11] A large herd of pigs was nearby, feeding on the hillside.

[31] The demons begged Jesus, "If you are going to drive us out, send us into that herd of pigs."

[12] The spirits begged Jesus, "Send us to the pigs, and let us go into them."

[32] "Go," Jesus told them; so they left and went off into the pigs. The whole herd rushed down the side of the cliff into the lake and were drowned.

[13] So he let them. The evil spirits went out of the man and went into the pigs. The whole herd—about two thousand pigs in all—rushed down the side of the cliff into the lake and were drowned.

[33] The men who had been taking care of the pigs ran away and went to the town, where they told the whole story, and what had happened to the men with the demons. [34] So everyone from the town went out to meet Jesus;

[14] The men who had been taking care of the pigs ran away and spread the news in the town and among the farms. The people went out to see what had happened. [15] They came to Jesus and saw the man who used to have the mob of demons in him. He was sitting there, clothed and in his right mind; and they were all afraid. [16] Those who had seen it told the people what had happened to the man with the demons, and about the pigs.

and when they saw him they begged him to leave their territory.

[17] So they began to ask Jesus to leave their territory.

There is little doubt that the event actually happened in very much the manner that Mark describes it, including the rather awkward detail about Jesus allowing the destruction of a herd of pigs. Why does Jesus allow something that so upsets the townspeople? Why does Mark include this story at this point in his Gospel?

The purpose of demonic possession is to distort and destroy what God has given to us, i.e., his own image and likeness (Gn 1:26). (The motion picture "The Exorcist" provides a rather gruesome portrayal of what demonic possession can do to a person.) Jesus appears on the scene to restore the work of the creator, to restore the divine likeness in his people. Nevertheless, Jesus performs his mission in a situation where the self-destructive power of evil is not yet completely removed.

The miracle which Jesus performs, he performs not only for the possessed man but also for the parabolic instruction of those around him. The destruction of the pigs is unfortunate but it is as nothing compared to the reality of God's Kingdom which has entered the life of the man once possessed. Their destruction does, however, demonstrate the already and not yet nature of the Kingdom of God.

Mark includes this story here for many reasons. First, it affords him an opportunity to remind us, through the cries of the demons (5:7), of just who Jesus really is. The demons' knowledge is set in contrast to the disciples' lack of understanding in the previous story (4:41). Second, it allows him to show Jesus actually bringing the Good News to the Gentiles prior to his final rejection at home (6:1-6). Third, it allows him to show the reaction of the townspeople to Jesus' proclamation in deed. In their self-centered perception of this parabolic proclamation they see only their loss of livelihood and fail completely to grasp the Good News of the Kingdom. Finally, Mark inserts this story here as part of his development of the role of the disciples. They hear Jesus' parables. They see his calming of the storm. They witness his dramatic expulsion of the demons and the destruction of the herd of pigs. Are they, however, really any different from the townspeople who are mainly concerned with their pigs? We shall soon find out.

c. Jairus' Daughter and the Woman with Severe Bleeding, 5:21–43

We have here the second example of intercalation in Mark's Gospel (see 3:20–35). The story about the woman with severe bleeding (5:25–34) is inserted between two sections of the story about Jairus' daughter (5:21–24, 35–43). The main point in both of these stories is faith. We are presented with the initial faith of Jairus (5:23), the somewhat mistaken faith of the woman (5:28), and, finally, with the apparent death of his daughter, a real challenge to the faith of Jairus (5:36), a challenge which he apparently rose to meet.

Many people had seen and heard about Jesus' miraculous healings. They were frequently performed by his touching the sick person, e.g., Simon's mother-in-law (1:31) and the leper (1:41) (see also 7:32; 8:23, 25). Many people came to believe in Jesus' miraculous powers but failed to see the real message of the Good News. Their faith was tinged with magic and confined to a concern for physical well-being. They believed, correctly, that contact with Jesus would enable them to share in the power he brought but they failed to appreciate the full meaning of that power.

Jairus first manifests this weak faith when he asks:

> *My little daughter is very sick. Please come and place your hands on her, so that she will get well and live (5:23).*

The woman with severe bleeding has a similar magical notion which, in her thinking, has extended even to Jesus' clothing:

> *If I touch his clothes . . . I shall get well (5:28).*

In contrast to Jairus and the woman who believe that contact with Jesus will bring healing benefits, the disciples are presented as still very much in the dark. When Jesus realizes that someone with faith in him has shared in the power of the Kingdom he asks: "Who touched my clothes?" (5:30). To the disciples this question is foolish, and they cannot understand why he would ask. They still do not realize that in him the power of God's Kingdom is a reality (5:31).

Jesus, however, could not let the woman go with her limited faith. He talks with her and gives her an opportunity to express her belief: "she . . . told him the whole truth" (5:33). Jesus, then, corrected her mistaken notions. It was not the touch that healed her; it was her faith. Her touch had put her, with her limited faith, in contact with Jesus, but it was her faith that had made her well (5:34).

All the while that this inserted incident is going on, Jairus is with Jesus. Now Jairus hears that his daughter is dead. Does he have faith? Jesus had never brought a dead person to life. Can Jairus go beyond the conviction that Jesus' touch will heal and really believe in Jesus? Jesus' challenge to Jairus is set in deliberate parallel to his rebuke to the disciples during the storm at sea.

Why are you frightened? Are you still without faith? (4:40).

Don't be afraid, only believe (5:36).

To heighten the contrast and continue developing the role of the disciples, Jesus brings only Peter, James and John into the house to witness the faith of Jairus and the life of his daughter. When Mark tells us "she got up at once" he uses the same Greek word he will use in each of the three passion predictions when speaking of Jesus' resurrection, the same Greek word he will also use after the transfiguration when Jesus says to these same three disciples:

Don't tell anyone what you have seen, until the Son of Man has risen from death (9:9).

The contrast Mark is drawing between the disciples and those healed in these two miracle stories is also indicated by his use of the number twelve. The woman had suffered for twelve years (5:25), while Jairus' daughter was twelve years old (5:42).

D. FAITH AND REJECTION, 6:1–6

This third section of Mark's Gospel (3:7–6:6) concludes in a manner parallel to the conclusion of the previous section (3:1–6). There Jesus is rejected by the Pharisees and Herodians; here Jesus is rejected even by the people he grew up with. Even with the slowness of the twelve really to understand Jesus, this final passage confirms the need for establishing a new people of God.

Here we see Jesus making his final visit to a synagogue on a Sabbath. As on the first occasion when he taught in a synagogue the people were amazed (1:22; 6:2). Here, however, they raise again the question of the source of his power. Unlike the Pharisees who think he is in league with Satan, and unlike his relatives who think he is insane, his townspeople simply cannot believe that he is really any different from themselves. They are not guilty of blasphemy; they are simply lacking in faith, even the kind of magical faith first had by Jairus and the woman with severe bleeding. His townspeople "rejected him" (6:4). The passage then concludes with a rather powerful observation:

He was not able to perform any miracles there (6:5).

This statement is the clearest assertion yet that Jesus is not a miracle-worker. Everything Jesus says and does is a proclamation of the Good News of the Kingdom. Miracles, however, as veiled manifestations of the Kingdom, can only succeed as proclamations where there is already some faith. To perform a miracle in the total absence of faith would be counter-productive. It would simply solidify the view that Jesus was a miracle-worker and nothing more.

The Good News is now in much sharper focus. Its scope is extended, though its appreciation by the multitude is still very shallow, as is its appreciation by the disciples. Mark has, however, set in motion Jesus' deliberate intent to reveal the full reality of the Good News first to the disciples and then to us.

STUDY QUESTIONS

1. Why did Jesus choose twelve apostles? Why did he do it on a mountain?

2. Do we claim to be members of God's people? What is more important: being born into a Christian family, being chosen by God, our faith relationship with Jesus, or our doing the will of God?

3. Why does Jesus use so many different images to describe the Kingdom of God? Why does he teach in parables? Can we expect to understand Jesus' teaching?

4. Can we see our own situation in one of the explanations of the sower parable (4:13–20)?

5. Do we see and hear the great truths about God's love, mercy and generosity in the people and events around us? Do the words of Isaiah apply to us (4:12)? Do we judge by our standards or by God's (4:24)?

6. In times of trouble is our faith strong or weak? Do we turn to Jesus and rely on him or do we become frightened and angry about our difficulties (4:40; 5:36)?

Chapter Four

JESUS AND HIS DISCIPLES

SUMMARY. As Mark continues to unfold the Good News of salvation two things become increasingly clear: first, the Good News is inseparable from the person of Jesus; second, the disciples fail to understand the real meaning of the Good News.

In this chapter we will see Jesus sending forth the disciples to learn by experience the ways of the Kingdom of God. They will succeed in their ministry but they will fail to learn.

We will also see Jesus, through a series of parabolic acts, attempting to open the ears and eyes of his disciples. By multiplying loaves and walking on water he points to the presence of God's Kingdom. He shows that the real Good News consists in the giving of self for others.

The disciples hear and see but fail to understand. It is not the disciples but a deaf and dumb man who hears. It is not the disciples but a blind man who sees. We who have ears and eyes, we who have the gift of faith, can still misunderstand. Let us listen carefully as Mark unfolds the Good News of salvation.

READ 6:6–8:26

OVERVIEW. In the fourth and final section of the first half of Mark's Gospel the unfolding of the Good News is brought to a head with the failure of the disciples to understand what it is that Jesus is doing. In the previous section (3:7—6:6) we saw Jesus giving privileged instruction to his disciples while indicating that his mission was universal in scope. In this section the universal scope of his mission is explicitly announced and acted upon; Jesus concentrates his attention even more on instructing the disciples, and, most significantly, the disciples are openly criticized for their failure to understand.

The activities of Jesus included in this section are carefully arranged to illustrate Mark's theological concerns. We will see Jesus moving back and forth across Lake Galilee and in and out of Gentile territory. An attempt to chart his movements on a map will prove exceedingly difficult. We will profit more from our reading of Mark if we attend more to the theological significance of the locales in which we find Jesus.

We will also notice a number of striking parallels both between passages within this section and between passages in this and other sections. Jesus' walking on the water (6:45–52) relates to his previous calming of the sea (4:35–41). His healing of the blind man at Bethsaida (8:22–26) relates to his subsequent cure of the blind man at Jericho (10:46–52). Most remarkable, however, are the two parallel sequences of events that form the main structural elements in this section. After an introduction involving the twelve, Herod and John the Baptist, the two main sections can be laid out in parallel columns as follows:

6:30–44	Miracle of Loaves	8:1–9
6:45–56	Crossing of Lake	8:10
7: 1–30	Discussions Involving Bread	8:11–21
7:31–37	Deaf—Cure—Blind	8:22–26

This entire section is a sequence of events drawn from Jesus' life and carefully arranged by Mark to portray the nature of Jesus' parabolic teaching and its effect on the disciples. We cannot help being reminded of the words Jesus quoted from the prophet Isaiah in explaining the purpose of parables:

That they may look and look,
    yet not see,

> They may listen and listen,
>   yet not understand
> for if they did, they would turn to God
>   and he would forgive them (4:12).

A. INTRODUCTION, 6:6–29

1. Mission of the Twelve, 6:6–13

Each of the four sections in the first half of Mark's Gospel begins with a summary statement about Jesus' activity. (Notice, however, that for smoothness and continuity the ending of one section and the beginning of the next often overlap.)

> Jesus went to Galilee and preached the Good News from God. . . .
> (1:14–15).

> He travelled all over Galilee, preaching in the synagogues and
> driving out demons (1:39).

> Jesus and his disciples went away to Lake Galilee and a large
> crowd followed him. . . . (3:7–12).

> Jesus went to the villages around there, teaching the people (6:6).

Each of the four sections also includes a call to discipleship, usually coming immediately after the summary statement about Jesus' activity (1:16–20; 2:14; 3:13–19; 6:7–13). In the first two sections Jesus was simply gathering followers to be with him. In the third section he sets aside twelve to be especially intimate with him, i.e., to receive the secret of the Kingdom. Here in the fourth section these twelve are sent out to learn, by personal experience, the reality of God's Kingdom.

The instructions Jesus gives them are designed to intensify this learning experience. He gave them the authority which he himself had as Son of God to continue the conquest of the Kingdom of Satan (6:7). He then sent them off two by two in absolute poverty (6:8–9). A great danger facing all ministers of the Gospel is that they can falsely attribute to themselves the successes they achieve. The presence of a companion in the Lord and the absence of any material support helps one to recognize the power of God in whatever good one achieves.

The details of the instruction on poverty differ slightly but significantly from what we find in Matthew's Gospel.

Mt 10:9–10	Mk 6:8–9
Do not carry any gold, silver, or copper *money* in your pockets; do not carry a *beggar's bag* for the trip, or an *extra shirt,* or *shoes,* or a *walking stick.*	Don't take anything with you on the trip *except* a walking stick; no *bread,* no beggar's bag, no money in your pockets. *Wear* sandals but don't wear an extra shirt.

The main idea, that they are to set out in a condition of genuine poverty, is identical in both. Mark's account, however, while repeating the five items italicized in Matthew, allows rather than forbids two of them, a walking stick and sandals. Mark also forbids an additional item, bread.

Mark has adapted this incident to introduce the final section of the first half of his Gospel, the final period of learning and testing prior to the revelation that will begin at Caesarea Philippi (8:27). It is deliberately designed to recall the condition of the Hebrew people setting out from Egypt to be led through the desert and fed with the bread from heaven. On the night before the exodus they were instructed to eat the passover lamb as follows:

> *In this manner you shall eat it: Your loins girded, your* sandals *on your feet, and your* staff *in your hand (Ex 12:11).*

The final instruction which Jesus gives the disciples is also designed to teach them that it is God's word they are preaching, not their own. They are told to preach their message quickly and leave if it is not accepted (6:10–11). Their responsibility is to be true to their mission; the responsibility for the outcome of their work rests with God alone.

We see them, at the end of this passage (6:12–13), actually engaged in the mission of preaching and healing. We will later see them returning to Jesus and reporting on their success (6:30). We will also see them, however, like the Hebrew nation before them, failing to see the hand of God in what is accomplished.

2. Herod's Fears, 6:14–16

The successes of the twelve further enhanced the reputation of Jesus. Herod heard about what was going on but he, like so many others, failed to grasp the full reality of what was happening. Various opinions are voiced about who Jesus is: John the Baptist, Elijah, a prophet. These same opinions will be repeated at the beginning of the next section (8:28). Here, however, they serve a double purpose.

First, these erroneous opinions serve to introduce this section (6:6—8:26) in which Jesus tries to communicate himself to his disciples. Second, Herod's fear that Jesus is really John the Baptist come back to life serves to introduce the following passage on the death of John.

3. Death of John the Baptist, 6:17–29

Sometime earlier Herod had executed John. The story is told here with a wealth of detail that most scholars recognize as pointing to historical accuracy. What is significant for us, however, is why Mark includes this story as part of his introduction to the two parallel loaves—healing sequences.

The two sequences which follow are a final effort on the part of Jesus to proclaim, by his actions, the reality of God's Kingdom; a reality first realized in Jesus himself. His proclamation will continue to meet with opposition and blindness even on the part of his disciples, an opposition and blindness which will eventually lead to his own execution.

Here Mark tells the story of John's execution, itself a story about opposition and blindness. John prefigures Jesus at the beginning of the Gospel (1:2–14). He will be used as a figure of Jesus again in the next section:

> *Elijah does indeed come first to get everything ready. Yet why do the Scriptures say that the Son of Man must suffer much and be rejected? I tell you, however, that Elijah has already come, and*

that people did to him what they wanted to, just as the Scriptures say about him (9:12–13).

Here Mark prefigures the fate that awaits Jesus with the story about John's execution. It serves as an urgent appeal to us the readers not to be deaf and blind, but to hear and see the Good News proclaimed by Jesus' words and deeds in the following two sequences.

B. LET THEM HEAR, 6:30—7:37

OVERVIEW. The twelve who had been sent out to preach now return to Jesus and report on their successes. Now Jesus, through a series of parabolic deeds and words, attempts to correct and refine their understanding of what God's Kingdom is all about.

1. Parabolic Actions, 6:30–56

a. The Five Thousand, 6:30–44

This story is the second of the nature miracles found in Mark's Gospel. Like the first, it is a parabolic action designed to tease those who see into it a deeper realization of what God's Kingdom is all about. The parallel with Exodus is deliberate and clear (Ex 16:12–35): the desert place, the complaint about the lack of food, the miraculous provision. The twelve baskets the disciples gather at the end are a further allusion to the twelve tribes of the new people of God. We the readers see all of this and more, but we will also see the disciples failing to understand the Good News of the Kingdom.

The story begins with a significant development in Jesus' attitude toward the crowds that are following him. He tries to avoid them! Crowds had been a problem since early in Mark's Gospel, e.g., the men who carried the paralytic had to make a hole in the roof (2:4). Until now, however, Jesus had attended to the needs of the crowd even at the expense of his own physical well-being. Now, however, when Jesus is so pressured by the crowds that he is unable to eat, he tries to avoid them. Thus far almost everyone has failed to appreciate the true nature of the Good News Jesus is

preaching. He now tries to concentrate on the twelve in the hope that at least they will understand him.

A further problem which begins to surface in this section concerns a kind of positive misunderstanding which results in misguided enthusiasm. Herod's fear about Jesus, whoever he was, was that people would raise him up to be their king. Jesus' fear about the people was that they would do precisely what Herod feared they would do. He therefore tries to avoid the crowd but their enthusiasm is such that they catch up with him (6:33).

At this point Mark adapts the story in a manner slightly different from what we see in Matthew.

Mt 14:14	Mk 6:34
Jesus got out of the boat, and when he saw the large crowd his heart was filled with pity for them, and he healed their sick.	When Jesus got out of the boat, he saw this large crowd, and his heart was filled with pity for them, because they were like sheep without a shepherd. So he began to teach them many things.

For Mark, Jesus sees the crowd as a flock of misguided sheep. Jesus, therefore, does not work additional miracles and risk leading them into a more serious misunderstanding. Instead, he teaches them and tries to correct their misunderstandings. What he taught we do not know, but the dialogue with the disciples which follows (6:35–37) indicates that even they remained very weak in understanding.

The actual account of the miraculous multiplication of the loaves contains two features of special significance. First, there is the deliberate and repetitious use of the word "all" by which Mark again indicates the universal scope of what Jesus is accomplishing:

> *They went from* all *the towns and ran ahead by land (6:33).*

> *Jesus then told his disciples to make* all *the people divide into groups (6:39).*

> *He also divided the fish among them* all *(6:41).*

That the use of "all" is a deliberate theological addition made by Mark is evident from the fact that neither Matthew nor Luke, both of whom include this story, has any of these three uses of "all" (see Mt 14:13–21; Lk 9:10–17).

Second, if we compare 6:41 with 14:22, another remarkable feature of this story becomes apparent.

6:41	14:22
Then Jesus took the five loaves and the two fish,	While they were eating Jesus took the bread,
looked up to heaven, and gave thanks to God.	gave a prayer of thanks,
He broke the loaves	broke it,
and gave them to his disciples to distribute to the people.	and gave it to his disciples. "Take it," he said, "this is my body."

What Mark has done is to deliberately use the same language in both accounts so that we the readers can hear what the disciples fail to hear. The Kingdom of God, first manifested in the person of Jesus, involves the ability to respond to the needs of others. What appears on the surface is an almost magical multiplication of bread. What is really involved, however, is a total dedication of self to the service of others, a total giving of self which in Jesus' case will be sacramentalized in the Eucharist and realized on the cross.

b. Walking on Water, 6:45–52

In the previous section (3:7—6:6), after the parable discourse (4:1–34), Mark related the incident about Jesus calming the storm. He did so in order to show that the disciples had failed to grasp the meaning of the parables.

Why are you frightened? Are you still without faith (4:40)?

Later in that section Mark used the example of Jairus as a contrast to the disciples.

Don't be afraid, only believe (5:36).

Here, again, Mark relates a nature miracle on the lake to illustrate the failure of the disciples to grasp the meaning of the miracle of the loaves, a parabolic action. Once again the disciples "were terrified" (6:50). They reacted as they did "because they had not understood what the loaves of bread meant; their minds could not grasp it" (6:52).

This second parabolic action includes a further revelation about the person of Jesus, a revelation which the disciples are also unable to grasp. When Jesus got into the boat he said:

It is I (6:50).

This type of expression is found in several places in the Old Testament:

God said to Moses, "I am Who I am" (Ex 3:14).

See now that I, even I am he, and there is no god besides me (Dt 32:39).

I the Lord, the first, and with the last; I am he (Is 41:4).

Jesus, then, is using a solemn expression for self-identification which in the sacred literature of the Jews was reserved for God alone. That Mark is deliberately presenting Jesus, in this parabolic action, as a manifestation of God himself is also indicated by the strange comment:

He was going to pass them by (6:48).

We were just told at the beginning of 6:48 that Jesus came out precisely because he saw that the disciples were having trouble. Why then would he pass them by? Here we have another deliberate allusion by Mark to the God of the Old Testament. On Mount Sinai God said to Moses:

I will make all my goodness pass before you, and will proclaim before you my name (Ex 32:19).

While my glory passes by I will put you in a cleft of the rock, and I will cover you with my hand until I have passed by (Ex 32:22).

Much later when Elijah encountered God on Mount Horeb we see the same expression being used:

And behold, the Lord passed by, and a great and strong wind rent the mountains and broke in pieces the rocks before the Lord (1 Kgs 19:11).

The Good News of the Kingdom of God is realized first in the person of Jesus. But who is Jesus? Understanding the Good News requires understanding the real identity of Jesus. Almost as in a contemporary detective story the readers or audience know the answer sooner than the characters in the story. While the disciples continue to lack understanding, Mark is unfolding for us, the readers, the real identity of Jesus.

c. Popularity at Gennesaret, 6:53–56

Lake Galilee was the meeting point of three territories: on the west was Galilee ruled by Herod Antipas; on the northeast was a largely Gentile region ruled by Herod's brother, Philip; on the southeast was the territory of the Ten Towns (the Decapolis) which was almost entirely Gentile and under direct Roman rule.

At the beginning of the first parabolic action we saw Jesus trying to avoid the Galilean crowds (6:31–32). At the beginning of the second action Jesus intended to leave Galilee altogether and go to Bethsaida which was in the Tetrarchy of Philip (6:45). The wind and Jesus' concern for his disciples prevented that crossing, however, and we see Jesus, at the beginning of this third parabolic action, back in Galilee, landing at Gennesaret.

What is surprising and significant in this incident is that Jesus remains entirely passive. He has taught and worked miracles but most have failed to understand him. Now, as the crowds press upon him, he behaves almost like the ghost the disciples thought he was in the previous story (6:49). This mysterious manifestation of God remains quietly aloof in the midst of the crowd. He does not preach nor teach nor work miracles. As God's Son, however, in whom the power of God's Kingdom is already realized, he cannot help allowing the power of that Kingdom to extend to those who touch him with even the weakest faith.

2. Teaching, 7:1–23

OVERVIEW. Jesus is intending to enter Gentile territory. Forced by circumstances back into Jewish territory, he remains quiet and passive. The Pharisees, however, provoke a new conflict to which Jesus responds by insisting that the Good News does not consist in what is superficial but rather in what touches the core of one's being. The teaching in this passage moves from a refutation of the Pharisees' objection to a parabolic teaching given to the crowd and finally to a more specific teaching given to the disciples.

For Mark this passage is an essential part of the sequence which begins with the feeding of the five thousand (6:30–44) and concludes with the healing of the deaf man (7:31–37). Mark indicates the connection of this passage with the miracle of the loaves by his repeated use of the Greek word for bread in this sequence (6:30—7:37). Our version obscures this connection by translating the word variously as "bread," "loaves" and "food."

How much bread *do you have (6:38)?*

Then Jesus took the five loaves *(6:41).*

They had not understood what the loaves of bread *meant (6:52).*

His disciples were eating food *with unclean hands (7:2).*

It isn't right to take the children's food *(7:27).*

More striking, however, and more important for Mark's purposes is the connection of this passage with the story of the healing of the deaf man. This entire sequence (6:30—7:37) is presented as a parabolic expression of the words from Is 6:9 which Mark quoted earlier:

They may listen and listen,
yet not understand (4:12).

After the controversy with the Pharisees Jesus will turn to the crowd and say:

Listen to me, all of you, and understand (7:14).

When the disciples ask him to explain the words he spoke to the crowds he will rebuke them with the words:

Don't you understand (7:18)?

The themes of hearing and understanding are then given their final parabolic expression when Jesus opens the ears of the deaf man at the end of the sequence (7:31–37).

a. Teaching of the Ancestors, 7:1–13

In addition to the Law of Moses there was a set of unwritten laws considered to have been handed down by word of mouth from earliest times. These laws were not just additional practices like the Monday and Thursday fast observed by the Pharisees. They were, rather, considered to be as binding on all Jews as the Law of Moses itself. One such law concerned washing before eating, a law the disciples were violating. When the Pharisees confront Jesus with this violation, Jesus, for the first time in Mark's Gospel, goes on the offensive. He deals with their complaint by making two even more serious complaints against the Pharisees themselves.

First, he accuses them of hypocrisy, a startling charge to make against men recognized for their rigorous religious observance. Jesus' complaint, however, is not that their deeds are inconsistent with their words. Jesus is trying to get people to see beyond the superficiality of deeds. The Pharisees, he charges, are so taken up with external actions that they have lost sight of the very foundation of their relationship with God. He attacks them with a quotation from Is 29:13:

> *These people, says God, honor me with their words*
> *but their heart is really far away from me (7:6).*

Second, Jesus proves his charge and, at the same time, demonstrates the inadequacy of the Pharisees' legalistic approach. He shows how, by their observance of the teaching on "Corban," they violate the real intention of the Law of Moses. As we pointed out in chapter two, any code of laws is inadequate, even the Law of Moses. What is really important is that the heart of man be in harmony with the will of God.

According to Nm 30:2 a promise or a vow made to God could not, under any circumstances, be broken. According to the teaching of the ancestors it was possible to vow or promise one's property to God and still retain the use of it. Having promised it to God, however, they could not give it to anyone else. Today we see people using similar techniques to avoid paying income or inheritance taxes. In Jesus' day this practice allowed people to avoid helping their elderly parents. Jesus' charge is that a superficial, legalistic approach to religious observances leaves one with intolerable contradictions and ultimately results in a failure to see and do the will of God.

b. What Is Unclean, 7:14–23

In 3:1–6 we saw the Pharisees reject Jesus as being inconsistent with their way of life. Here we see Jesus reject the Pharisees as being inconsistent with the Kingdom of God. Jesus turns instead to the crowd and teaches them, as he had taught them before, with a parable. This passage bears many similarities to the passage on the sower in Mk 4:

4:1–2	a crowd	7:14
4:3	Listen!	7:14
4:3–8	parable	7:15
4:10–12	alone with disciples	7:17
4:13	failure to understand	7:18
4:14–20	explanation	7:18–23

There are, however, two significant differences which indicate the developments that have occurred in Mark's presentation of the Good News. First, Jesus' call to the crowds in 4:3 is simply "Listen!" In 7:14, however, it is expanded: "Listen to me, all of you, and understand." The addition of "to me" focuses on the identity of Jesus as being essential to an understanding of the Good News. The addition of "all of you" points in the direction of universality. The addition of "understand" gives greater emphasis to Mark's fundamental concern in this sequence.

Second, in 7:18 Jesus not only observes the failure of the disciples to understand, as he did in 4:13, but he also delivers a positive rebuke:

You are no more intelligent than the others (7:18).

Mark is building up to the climax of the first half of his Gospel, the tragic failure of the disciples, with all their privileged instruction, really to understand Jesus' proclamation of the Good News.

The parable which Jesus speaks to the crowd in 7:14 responds to the Pharisees' concern about cleanliness and also intensifies Jesus' concern about what is really important, what lies in the heart of man. He shifts the discussion, however, from the topic of clean hands to the topic of clean foods, a matter clearly spelled out in the Law of Moses. Jesus totally rejects any law of superficialities and declares that nothing outside the heart of man is unclean.

The parable itself is a parable of the Kingdom pointing to a reality which cannot be expressed in words. Jesus' explanation to the disciples, then, is again only an attempt to lead them a little further in appreciating the reality of God's Kingdom. If one lives in God's Kingdom, then everything is as God wants it to be and nothing is unclean. If one does not live in God's Kingdom, then all kinds of disorders will appear in the very heart of man and that is what is really unclean.

3. The Woman at Tyre, 7:24–30

Jesus finally succeeds in leaving Jewish territory. He goes to the region of Tyre, a Phoenician city on the Mediterranean about thirty-five miles from Gennesaret. There Mark shows him performing a miracle which continues the universality theme introduced with the multiplication of loaves. In Galilee Jesus had satisfied the needs of "all" the people (6:33, 39, 41). Does this "all" include Gentiles as well as Jews? The faith of the woman leads Jesus to respond in the affirmative and paves the way for the feeding of the four thousand in Gentile territory (8:1–9).

The words and images which Mark uses in telling this story are intended to help us follow his unfolding of the Good News. We are told that Jesus tried to remain hidden (7:24) because people had failed to understand him and were seeking him for the wrong reasons. Mark, however, adds: "but he could not stay hidden" (7:24). In the parable of the lamp he had said:

> *What is hidden away will be brought out into the open, and whatever is covered up will be uncovered (4:22).*

Jesus is hiding because people have failed to understand him. As we move into the second half of Mark's Gospel (8:27—16:8), however, Jesus' real identity will be uncovered for all to see.

In spite of his seclusion the mother of a girl with an evil spirit learns of his presence. Her approach to Jesus reminds us of the incident with Jairus:

> *When he saw Jesus he threw himself down at his feet and begged him. . . . (5:22–33).*

> *A certain woman . . . came to him at once and fell at his feet. . . . She begged Jesus. . . . (7:25–26).*

In both cases persons of faith were reaching out for the power of God's Kingdom. In the case of the woman at Tyre, however, we are told explicitly that she "was a foreigner" (7:26).

Finally there is the connection which Mark makes with the miracle of the loaves. The dialogue between Jesus and the mother contains two important ideas:

> *It isn't right to take the children's* food *and throw it to the dogs (7:27).*

> *Even the dogs under the table eat the children's* leftovers *(7:28).*

The word used here for "food" is the same word used for "bread" and "loaves" in the story of the five thousand (6:30–44). In that miracle we were told:

> *The disciples took up twelve* baskets *full of what was* left *of the* bread *and of the fish (6:43).*

Twelve baskets is enough to satisfy the needs of the new people of God.

4. Cure of the Deaf Mute, 7:31–37

People with ears to hear, especially the disciples, have failed to understand the proclamation of Jesus. Now Jesus, in Gentile territory, turns to a man without hearing and gives him the power to hear. The opening verse describes, very compactly, a journey through many Gentile regions. Sidon is almost twenty miles north of Tyre while the territory of the Ten Towns is southeast of Lake Galilee. The journey would have been well over a hundred miles and could have taken weeks. Mark is here indicating the availability of God's Kingdom to those outside the house of Israel.

The miracle story itself is somewhat different from the other miracle stories we have seen. This story and the cure of the blind man at Bethsaida (8:22–26) are the only healing miracles in Mark not found in any other Gospel. Both stories place great emphasis on the details of Jesus' words and actions. Neither story has any mention of faith or any indication of the presence of evil power. Both stories are presented by Mark as parabolic actions. They bring to a climax Jesus' proclamation of the Good News in the first half of the Gospel. They illustrate the failure of the disciples to hear and see the full reality of what Jesus is accomplishing. They fulfill the words spoken by the prophet Isaiah:

> *Then the eyes of the blind shall be opened,*
> *and the ears of the deaf unstopped (Is 35:5).*

C. LET THEM SEE, 8:1–26

1. The Four Thousand, 8:1–9

Still in the Gentile territory of the Ten Towns, Jesus is once again confronted by a large crowd who have had nothing to eat. Again he works a miracle, feeding four thousand with a few loaves and fish. This story is very similar to the first multiplication of loaves and fish (6:30–44) but differs in a number of significant ways.

In both stories Jesus has compassion on the crowd. In the first he has compassion because they are like misguided sheep; they are following Jesus for the wrong reasons (6:34). His compassion there leads him to teach them. In the second story it is precisely because they are hungry that he has compassion on them (8:2). In this story, then, there is no indication that he suspects them of following him for the wrong reasons.

In the first story the crowd had been with Jesus for only a day and had come from the towns in that immediate region (6:33). In the second story the crowd had been with Jesus for three days and some had come from a great distance (8:3). People had been joining Jesus all along his journey through Gentile territory. Here on the southeastern shore of Lake Galilee, after teaching them for three days, Jesus feeds them in a manner that again has strong eucharistic overtones.

Even after witnessing the first miracle of the loaves the disciples are again presented as not understanding Jesus' ability to feed his followers (8:4), a failure to understand which will soon be severely criticized (8:17–18). When Jesus asked how much bread they had in the first story, their response was "five loaves" (6:38). In this story it is "seven loaves" (8:5). The number seven appears again as the number of baskets of leftovers (8:9).

There is considerable disagreement among scholars on the meaning of these numbers. Some have suggested that in the first miracle, performed in Jewish territory, the twelve baskets symbolized the twelve tribes and the twelve apostles as leaders of the new Israel. In the second miracle the seven loaves and seven baskets would symbolize the seven leaders of the Greek-speaking Christians in Jerusalem (Acts 6:1–6). Whether or not this opinion is correct there is a final difference which clearly indicates that the first miracle concerns Jews and the second concerns Gentiles.

As we pointed out earlier the first miracle story is told with the same kind of terminology used in the account of the Last Supper. We find the same eucharistic terminology in the second miracle with one important difference. In 6:41 Jesus uses the same word for giving thanks to God that he will use in 14:22. In 8:6, however, he uses a different Greek word which is the same as the word Paul uses in his account of the Last Supper (1 Cor 11:24).

Loaves		Last Supper		
Mk 6:41	=	Mk 14:22	=	Mt 26:26
Mk 8:6	=	1 Cor 11:24	=	Lk 22:19

What most scholars agree upon is that Mark (and also Matthew) use the eucharistic terminology then current in Jewish Christian communities, while Paul (and also Luke) use the terminology of Gentile communities. Mark, then, in the second miracle, is deliberately adopting the Gentile eucharistic terminology.

Both stories are told in a liturgical framework. In both Jesus gives of himself to the people who follow him, first by teaching them and then by feeding them. One cannot help being struck by the final words of the second story, "Jesus sent the people away" (8:9). In today's liturgy the words are: "The Mass is ended, go in peace."

2. Teaching, 8:10–21

a. Pharisees Ask for a Sign, 8:10–13

As in the previous sequence, after the miracles of the loaves Jesus crosses Lake Galilee (8:10; see 6:45–52). This time he crosses from Gentile territory into Jewish territory only to conflict once again with the Pharisees. This time, however, we are told that "they wanted to trap him" (8:11). Mark uses the same word he used to refer to the temptation by Satan (1:13). He uses this word on only two other occasions in his Gospel: when the Pharisees try to trap him with the question on divorce (10:2), and when the Pharisees try to trap him with the question about paying taxes (12:15). The Pharisees, then, try to trap Jesus three times—here in Galilee (8:11), after he enters Judea (10:2), and finally after he has entered Jerusalem (12:13).

In this passage, which is part of the loaves-healing sequence concerned with seeing, they try to trap him by asking for a sign (8:11). They want to see some incontrovertible proof that he has

God's approval. They are asking for the same kind of proof that Satan was asking for in the first temptation in Matthew's Gospel:

> *If you are God's Son, order these stones to turn into bread (Mt 4:3).*

Jesus, however, will not yield to the temptations of either Satan or the Pharisees (8:12). He is true to himself. He is not a miracle-worker. He will not be tempted to win men's approval by being false to his mission to bring God's Kingdom to all. His response to the Pharisees is the second solemn affirmation to appear in Mark's Gospel:

> *No, I tell you! (Amen, I say to you!) No such proof will be given this people (8:12; see 3:28).*

The story ends with Jesus' leaving the Pharisees and crossing the lake back into Gentile territory (8:13). In the previous controversy (7:1–13) Jesus had taken the offensive against the Pharisees by charging them with hypocrisy. Now he turns his back on them, not to encounter them again until he enters Judea and Jerusalem for his final act of self-giving.

b. Yeast of the Pharisees and of Herod, 8:14–21

Like the teaching in the previous loaves—healing sequence (7:1–23), this passage is also connected with the multiplication of loaves by initiating the discussion on the topic of bread (8:14). It is likewise connected with the healing miracle which follows by the double admonition:

> *You have eyes—can't you see?*

> *You have ears—can't you hear (8:18)?*

Yeast is a symbol of corruptive power. When Jesus says "Be on your guard against the yeast of the Pharisees and the yeast of Herod" (8:15), he is speaking about a kind of corruption that could be common not only to the Pharisees and Herod but to the disciples as well. The corruption he is speaking of is the desire for earthly power, a desire already present among the Pharisees and Herod, a desire which will soon surface among the disciples as well (9:34; 10:37).

The Pharisees had already manifested this corruption by mis-understanding the true identity of Jesus, by thinking of him as a miracle-worker who would win the people away from them. The danger Jesus saw for the disciples was that they too might mis-take Jesus for a miracle-worker who would use his abilities to gain earthly power. So far the disciples had not misunderstood Jesus; they had simply failed to understand him. Even now they fail to understand the warning about the yeast of the Pharisees. Their concern for food blinded them from seeing Jesus as the Son of God who could nourish them with the life of God's Kingdom.

At this point Jesus delivers his most biting rebuke to the disci-ples. He scolds them for their blindness and tries to open their eyes. His rebuke, interestingly, consists of *seven* questions which summarize the two loaves—healing sequences up to this point.

[1] Why are you discussing about not having any bread (8:17)?

[2] Don't you know or understand yet (8:17)?

[3] Are your minds so dull (8:17)?

[4] You have eyes—can't you see?
You have ears—can't you hear (8:18)?

[5] Don't you remember (8:18)?

[6] When I broke the five loaves for the five thousand peo-ple how many baskets full of leftover pieces did you take up? ... and when I broke the seven loaves for the four thousand people ... how many baskets full of leftover pieces did you take up (8:19–20)?

[7] And you still don't understand (8:21)?

3. Cure of the Blind Man, 8:22–26

Jesus finally comes to Bethsaida, the city in the largely Gentile region ruled by Herod's brother, Philip. Jesus had intended to go there after the first multiplication of the loaves but was turned back by the storm (6:45–52). Now, at Bethsaida at last, he works his final miracle in the first half of Mark's Gospel.

This miracle, which completes the second loaves—healing sequence, is very similar to the healing of the deaf man (7:31–37). This miracle, however, is the only one in any of the Gospels in which a healing is accomplished in stages. As a parabolic action symbolizing the opening of eyes to see the reality which Jesus is bringing it fits perfectly Mark's plan for gradually unfolding the full reality of the Good News.

Up to this point in the Gospel the disciples have failed to understand what Jesus was proclaiming. What Jesus is proclaiming involves the identity of Jesus himself, for it is only because he is God's Son that he can bring God's Kingdom to men. As we enter the second half of Mark's Gospel, Jesus will begin gradually to reveal his own true identity to the disciples.

STUDY QUESTIONS

1. Why does Jesus encourage poverty? Is it possible for those with material wealth to do God's work? What difficulties will be encountered? How can these be overcome?

2. Do we understand the multiplication of the loaves? What is the connection between the loaves and the Eucharist? Between the loaves and the cross? What are the practical consequences for our lives today?

3. What is unclean in our lives? Do we tend to judge others and even ourselves on the basis of what is superficial? Are we any more intelligent than the disciples (7:18)?

4. Who is Jesus? He is a human being like us but he is obviously more. What do the stories of this section, the loaves, the walking on water and the Gentile mission, tell us about who Jesus is?

5. Do we see and hear the mysteries of salvation unfolding all around us? Are we blinded and deafened by the noises, disturbances and concerns of modern life? Can we think of something in recent weeks that we saw or heard but failed to understand?

Chapter Five

THE SUFFERING SON OF MAN

SUMMARY. Mark's Gospel can be divided into two halves which are connected by the central passage in which Peter confesses: "You are the Messiah" (8:29). Everything before this passage has been leading up to it, while everything after flows away from it.

As Mark continues to unfold the true nature of the Good News he points to the true identity of Jesus as a necessary element in the Good News. In this chapter we will consider the nature of Jesus as Messiah, as suffering Son of Man and as triumphant Son of Man.

We will also observe how the disciples' failure to understand intensifies. Now they positively misunderstand who Jesus is and what their relationship to him should be. At the end of this chapter we will see how this misunderstanding results in their failure to cast out a demon. How often are our failures as Christians due to our misunderstanding about who Jesus is and what he means for us?

READ 8:27–9:29

OVERVIEW. The second half of Mark's Gospel (8:27—16:8) consists of three main sections: first, Jesus foretells his passion three times and after each time he tries to correct the misunderstandings of his disciples (8:31—10:52); second, Jesus enters Jersusalem for his final confrontation with Judaism (11:1—13:37); third, Jesus fulfills his mission by his passion, death and resurrection (14:1—16:8).

The first of these sections is further divided into three parts, each beginning with a passion prediction and each following the same basic format:

	I	II	III
Passion Prediction	8:31–32	9:30–31	10:32–34
Misunderstanding	8:32–33	9:32–34	10:35–40
Instruction	8:34–9:1	9:35–37	10:41–45
Added Material	9:2–29	9:38–10:31	10:46–52

The first of these parts, the subject of this chapter, is preceded by the story of Peter's confession (8:27–30), a story which serves as a bridge connecting the two halves of Mark's Gospel.

In the first half of his Gospel Mark showed Jesus proclaiming the Good News of the Kingdom in parabolic words and deeds. Mark also showed the disciples failing to understand the reality of that Good News; they failed to see the true nature of God's Kingdom as it is first realized in the person of Jesus. In the second half of his Gospel Mark shows Jesus explaining the nature of the Kingdom by unfolding his own true identity. Mark also shows the disciples going beyond a mere lack of understanding and now positively misunderstanding the Good News.

Jesus' struggle with his disciples throughout the first half of the Gospel results in a breakthrough at Caesarea Philippi, that one glimmer of insight in Peter's confession. Immediately, however, this moment of understanding gives way to the misunderstandings which will later result in Judas' betrayal and Peter's denial.

A. PETER'S CONFESSION, 8:27–30

From Bethsaida, in the territory of Philip, Jesus and the twelve journeyed about twenty-five miles north to the city of Caesarea

Philippi, a city that had been rebuilt by Philip and renamed in honor of Caesar. Philip's territory was mostly Gentile, containing only a few thousand Jews recently settled there by Herod the Great. Nevertheless, Jews of Jesus' day considered Caesarea Philippi to be the northern limit of the Promised Land since it was located near the site of the ancient city of Dan.

> *Moses went up . . . to Mount Nebo. . . . And the Lord showed him all the land, Gilead as far as Dan. . . . And the Lord said to him, "This is the land of which I swore to Abraham. . . ."* (Dt 34:1–4).

At the turning point in Mark's Gospel Jesus must make a decision. Will he continue north and leave forever the people who had rejected him or will he travel south to Jersualem, the center of Judaism, and accept the fate that awaits him there? True to his identity, which he will shortly reveal, his decision will be to go south. Before revealing his own identity, however, he gives the disciples one last chance to manifest some understanding:

> *Tell me, who do people say I am (8:27)?*

> *What about you? Who do you say I am (8:29)?*

After the calming of the storm the disciples had wondered: "Who is this man?" (4:41). Later, in the section on Herod and the death of the Baptist, we saw a variety of opinions: John the Baptist, Elijah, a prophet (6:14–15). Here the opinions of the people have not changed (8:28), but the disciples, who had been given the secret of the Kingdom of God (4:11), show the first sign of understanding. Peter speaks for the rest of the disciples and says:

> *You are the Messiah (8:29).*

Peter is correct but only partially so. In a few verses we shall see how weak Peter's understanding really was. Since a half-truth is often more damaging than no truth, Jesus again commands silence:

> Do not tell anyone about me (8:30).

"Messiah" is the Hebrew name for the expected bringer of salvation. Literally, "messiah" means the anointed one. Samuel, under the direction of God, had anointed Saul and later David as kings over God's people (1 Sm 10:1; 16:13). For several centuries David's descendants ruled in Jerusalem until about six hundred years before Christ. Since then succeeding foreign empires had conquered and subjugated God's people.

The prophets and other writers in Israel's religious tradition had constantly foretold the coming of a savior who would free God's people. Typical of the passages which formed the popular ideas about the messiah is the following from the prophet Jeremiah:

> Behold, the days are coming, says the Lord, when I will raise up
> for David a righteous Branch, and he shall reign as king and
> deal wisely, and shall execute justice and righteousness in the
> land. In his day Judah will be saved, and Israel will dwell
> securely (Jer 23:5–6).

In Jesus' day the Romans ruled the entire region and many expected the messiah to appear at any time, ridding the land of oppression and re-establishing the throne of David. This popular notion of the messiah contained no hint that the savior would be God's Son and it was never free from nationalistic overtones.

Jesus was indeed the messiah of Jewish expectation but not according to the popular understanding. He therefore forbade the disciples to reveal his identity to anyone and began to teach them who he really was.

B. THE SON OF MAN, 8:31–9:1

OVERVIEW. Names are somewhat arbitrary. A rose by any other name would still smell the same. By repeated use, however, names become fixed in meaning and therefore limited in application. Whenever something new appears, a newly independent nation or a new invention, it is usually necessary to create a new name that will be free from the connotation, prejudice or bias of the old name. Often new understandings necessitate new names, e.g., many people today feel the word "chairman" has a built-in bias in favor of male leaders and prefer the word "chairperson."

When Jesus appeared on the scene there was no current name, word or title that was adequate to express every facet of his identity. To call Jesus the messiah may have been correct to a certain extent, but this title was so set in its meaning that it could only prevent people from grasping the full reality of Jesus. Jesus preferred the expression "Son of Man," an expression that was sufficiently vague and general for Jesus to redefine it and apply it to himself. In this passage the expression occurs twice, each time focusing on a different aspect of Jesus' identity.

> *The Son of Man must suffer much, and be rejected by the elders, the chief priests, and the teachers of the Law. He will be put to death, and after three days he will rise to life (8:31).*

> *. . . the Son of Man will be ashamed of him when he comes in the glory of his Father with the holy angels (8:38).*

Jesus has taken two different concepts from the Old Testament and combined them in his explanation of who the Son of Man is. From Deutero-Isaiah he has taken the idea of the suffering servant:

> *Behold my servant shall prosper, he shall be exalted and lifted up, and shall be very high (52:13). He was despised and rejected by men, a man of sorrows and acquainted with grief (53:3). He was wounded for our transgressions, he was bruised for our iniquities (53:5). He poured out his soul to death, and was numbered with the transgressors (53:12).*

From the book of Daniel Jesus has taken the idea of the apocalpytic Son of Man:

> *I saw in the night visions, and behold, with the clouds of heaven*
> *there came one like a son of man, and he came to the Ancient of*
> *Days and was presented before him. And to him was given*
> *dominion and glory and kingdom, that all peoples, nations, and*
> *languages should serve him; his dominion is an everlasting*
> *dominion, which shall not pass away, and his kingdom one that*
> *shall not be destroyed (7:14).*

For the people of Jesus' day it would have been easier to imagine a horseless carriage than to see the ruler from the end time as the suffering servant. Jesus, however, chose precisely this strange combination of ideas to reveal his own true identity.

1. First Passion Prediction, 8:31–32

The first passion prediction, quoted above (8:31), is also the first time in Mark's Gospel that Jesus departs from his veiled manner of speaking.

> *"He made this very clear to them" (8:32).*

What he made clear to them was that their understanding of "messiah" had to be corrected with an understanding of Jesus that embraced both majesty and lowliness. "Son of Man" is a title of both majesty and lowliness but the emphasis in each of the passion predictions is on the lowliness of the Son of Man, his suffering and death.

Much earlier Mark had told us that the Pharisees and Herodians made plans to kill Jesus (3:6). Both groups were jealous of their own authority over the people. Both saw Jesus as someone the people might regard as the messiah. Both decided to eliminate this threat, to kill Jesus. What Mark is telling us in this passion prediction, however, is new and different in two ways. First, Jesus is not the messiah of popular understanding but the Son of Man of lowliness and majesty. Second, Jesus will die but the reason for his death is much more profound than the jealousy of men. The very nature of the Son of Man is such that he *"must* suffer much" (8:31).

How his death will come about is significant but secondary to the fact that suffering and death are essential to the very nature of Jesus. His death will, however, be brought about by men, specifically "the elders, the chief priests, and the teachers of the Law" (8:31). These three groups comprise what is known as the Sanhedrin, the council in Jerusalem which governed the Jewish people in matters not reserved to the Roman authorities. Jesus' final rejection will come, then, not from individual Pharisees and Herodians but from the recognized leaders of all the Jews.

Coupled with the humiliation of the Son of Man, however, is the assurance of final victory. After the suffering, rejection and death he will rise. The mystery of Jesus involves dying and rising as two poles which together and only together can point to the full reality of God's Kingdom. Jesus does not die and then undo the damage by rising again. Rather, it is precisely in suffering and dying that he achieves the final and perfect victory over all the forces hostile to God's Kingdom. It is precisely through suffering and dying in perfect obedience to God's will that the new life of God's Kingdom is forever beyond the reach of the Kingdom of Satan.

An interesting feature of this passion prediction is the time reference which differs from what we find in Matthew and Luke:

Mt 16:21 (see Lk 9:22)	Mk 8:31
on the third day I will be raised to life.	after three days he will rise to life.

Matthew and Luke are speaking about the traditional three days: Good Friday, Holy Saturday, Easter Sunday. Mark, however, says "*after* three days." After the three days of suffering, rejection and death during which the perfection of God's Kingdom will be manifested in him, the new life of that Kingdom will appear.

Throughout his Gospel, as we have already seen (see comments on 3:22; 8:11), Mark makes careful use of the number three. This number had special religious significance not only among Jews but among Egyptians and Greeks as well. It suggested a completeness that somehow involved God. In Mark's Gospel the movement of Jesus toward his destiny is built on threes. People come to Jesus from Jerusalem three times (3:8; 3:22; 7:1). The

Pharisees try to trap Jesus three times (8:11; 10:2; 12:13). Jesus predicts his passion three times (8:31; 9:30; 10:32). Jesus enters Jerusalem three times on three successive days (11:11; 11:15; 11:27). After these three days of entry into Jerusalem Jesus begins his final three days of suffering, rejection and death (14:1—15:41). After these three climactic days the new life of God's Kingdom will finally be manifested and the eyes of the disciples will be opened. Mark does not tell us that this resurrection will happen on Sunday but only that on Sunday it has already happened (16:1–8).

2. Misunderstanding, 8:32–33

Peter is like the enthusiastic sports fan who sees his team winning by a wide margin in the final inning or period of play and then suddenly going down to defeat. He cannot believe his eyes! Peter was convinced that this powerful person he had been following, this person who healed the sick, drove out demons, walked on water and multiplied loaves, was the messiah. Jesus was the one who would assume the leadership of his people and drive out the Romans. Perhaps the greatest aspect of all of this for Peter, the fisherman, was that he was on the winning team. His enthusiasm, however, was cut short by the passion prediction. He just could not believe it. Immediately he protests:

So Peter took him aside and began to rebuke him (8:32).

What Peter said we do not know but it must have involved his insistence that suffering and dying was no way for the messiah to behave.

The structure Mark has given this passage (8:27–33) brings out the relationships among the differing responses to Jesus:

What do people say?
    What do you (disciples) say?
        Peter confesses
            Passion prediction
        Peter rebukes

Jesus turns to disciples
Your thoughts are men's thoughts

The rebuke, "Get away from me, Satan" (8:33), which Jesus delivers to Peter, is really delivered to all the disciples, for Peter was
their spokesman. The comment, "Your thoughts are men's
thoughts, not God's" (8:33), is similar to the words in an earlier
rebuke, "You are no more intelligent than the others" (7:17).
Though here their lack of understanding has become positive
misunderstanding, in both places their failures are equated with
those of the people as a whole. To think of Jesus as a political lib-
erator is just as erroneous, if not more so, as thinking of him as
Elijah or John the Baptist or a prophet.

Peter's (and the other disciples') refusal to accept a suffering
messiah indicates an inability to respond spontaneously to the
will of God. Even worse it indicates a desire to frustrate the divine plan for the salvation of mankind. Peter and the other disciples are not yet living the life of God's Kingdom. They are still
thinking the thoughts of men. They are still very much under the
influence of the Kingdom of Satan. One could even say that Peter, by trying to persuade Jesus to act like a political messiah, was
allying himself with Satan and becoming for Satan an agent of
temptation.

Let us not be too hasty to condemn Peter. How often do we,
even in prayer, try to get God to do things our way? How often
do we, even in prayer, close our minds to seeing the hand of God
in events that, at first sight, appear distasteful?

3. Discipleship, 8:34—9:1

Mark has told us, through the first passion prediction, what the
Good News means for the life of Jesus. Now he tells us, through a
series of five sayings of Jesus, what the Good News means for the
life of a disciple. To show that these sayings are intended for everyone and not just for the twelve Mark has Jesus addressing the
following words to a crowd:

[1] If anyone wants to come with me he must forget himself,
carry his cross, and follow me (8:34).

Coming with Jesus is what Christian discipleship is all about, but what does it really involve? First of all it involves self-denial. A true disciple is willing and able to recognize and admit his own inadequacy. He is then able to turn to Jesus and stake his life on him. To the extent that we affirm ourselves, living on the assumption that our perspectives are adequate and our abilities will suffice, to that extent we have denied our need for Jesus.

If we take our stand on Jesus, however, we can carry our cross and follow him. Here Mark is probably not speaking about the cross of crucifixion but about the cross as a mark of initiation (e.g., the cross traced on the chest at baptism; see also Ez 9:4). Not until 15:13 does Mark make any mention of the crucifixion; before that point we are simply told that Jesus will suffer and die. The person who has been initiated into Christian discipleship must not only be with Jesus but must bear the mark of discipleship and everything implied by that mark, even to the point of suffering and death.

In bearing the mark of our discipleship we are never alone. Whatever we may be called to endure Jesus has already endured. In fact, it is precisely because Jesus has already suffered and died that we are able to bear the mark of our commitment to him. He does not ask us to chart new courses, to initiate new kinds of suffering. He only asks us to follow him (8:34).

[2] Whoever wants to save his own life will lose it; but whoever loses his life for me and for the gospel will save it (8:35).

This second saying repeats the main point of the first saying, i.e., that discipleship involves staking one's life on Jesus. It adds, however, three additional ideas. First, discipleship involves a reversal of values: the only way to save one's life is to lose it. When we guard and protect our own way of seeing things and doing things, when we trust in ourselves and no one else, when we make ourselves the ultimate judge of our own affairs, then we are enslaved, we have lost our lives. If, however, we are willing to let go, if we are willing to trust in Jesus, believing that God's ways are superior to men's ways, if we stake our lives on Jesus, then we are free, we are alive.

The second idea which Mark develops here is that Jesus is present in and identified with the Good News. The disciple is called upon to lose his life "for me and for the gospel" (8:35). In the first half of Mark's Gospel Jesus proclaimed the Good News in his words and deeds. There were only a couple of places (e.g., 7:14) where we caught a hint that the identity of Jesus was involved in the Good News. In the second half Jesus unfolds his own true identity as a necessary element in the unfolding of the Good News. In this saying (8:35) we see, for the first time, an explicit statement that Jesus is to be identified with the Good News. We are not called upon to lose our lives just for a person, nor just for the message he announces, but rather for the message he announces which is already realized in and identified with his person.

The final idea which appears in this saying (8:35) is the certainty of the life that is saved. He who tries to set himself up as master in his own little kingdom has already lost whatever small share of life he may have had (see 4:25). He who stakes his life on Jesus has surrendered his life but has actually just begun to live the life of God's Kingdom. Losing one's life for Jesus and the Gospel means that one's life already belongs to God. God will stand by that life, nourishing it and increasing it beyond our wildest expectations.

As we mentioned in chapter one, faith always involves a risk. How much we should be willing to risk for Jesus and the Gospel is the topic of the third saying:

> [3] Does a man gain anything if he wins the whole world and loses his life? Of course not! There is nothing a man can give to regain his life (8:36–37).

Having suggested in the previous saying (8:35) that our lives in God's Kingdom are vastly more important than our worldly lives, Mark now asks how much even these worldly lives are worth. The implication is that we would be willing to risk everything to save our worldly lives. For the sake of living in God's Kingdom, then, we should be willing to risk even more, even our worldly lives. Jesus will suffer and die. To follow him is to risk the same fate.

What will happen if we are unwilling to risk everything? What will happen if we are uncomfortable following a messiah who has to suffer and die?

> [4] If, then, a man is ashamed of me and of my teaching in this godless and wicked day, then the Son of Man will be ashamed of him when he comes in the glory of his Father with the holy angels (8:38).

Jesus had chosen the title "Son of Man" as a means of correcting the majestic messianic ideas of the disciples. This lowly Son of Man would rise to life after his three days of suffering, rejection and death. Only here, however, do we get our first glimpse of the full glory of the Son of Man. Three times Mark will show us the glory of the Son of Man (8:38; 13:26; 14:62). Only here, however, does he present the glorious Son of Man as he who will pass judgment in the end time.

It is significant that the Son of Man does not come in his own glory but instead in the glory of his Father. If we work to achieve our own glory we will accomplish nothing more than our own glory which, in the last analysis, is nothing. Jesus, by denying himself and subjecting himself in obedience, worked for the Father's glory and in the end shares fully in that glory.

> [5] Remember this! (Amen, I say to you!) There are some here who will not die until they have seen the Kingdom of God come with power (9:1).

We who have staked our lives on Jesus will also share in that glory, but when? In the last saying of this series, which is also the third solemn affirmation of the Gospel (see 3:28; 8:12), Mark is saying that some will experience this glory even in their own lifetime.

Is Jesus speaking of the actual parousia when the Son of Man will come to judge? This interpretation is highly unlikely, for elsewhere Mark shows Jesus saying:

> *No one knows, however, when that day or hour will come—*
> *neither the angels in heaven, nor the Son; only the Father knows*
> *(13:32).*

Most of us, with our weak faith, are still languishing in the misunderstandings that characterized the disciples. Some, however, even before they die will be brought to a union of heart and mind with the will of God. The classical spiritual writers have described this state as the "unitive way." Being God's Son, Jesus' mind and heart are already united to the will of God. He is inviting us to enter into God's family with him. He is assuring us that some of us, even before we die, will realize that intimacy with the will of God that he already has.

C. FULFILLMENT OF LAW AND PROPHETS, 9:2–13

1. Transfiguration, 9:2–9

> *Six days later Jesus took Peter, James and John with him, and led them up a high mountain by themselves. As they looked on, a change came over him (9:2).*

The "six days later" of the transfiguration is undoubtedly related to the six days in Jerusalem, the three days of entry and three days of suffering, rejection and death, before the resurrection. Here we have seen Jesus predicting the events that will lead to his death and after six days going up a high mountain to present the three disciples with a foretaste of the glory that will come. The mountain is not identified in the passage but is probably best viewed as being Mount Hermon, the highest mountain in the entire region and not far from Caesarea Philippi.

The story of the transfiguration is an essential part of this pivotal section in the center of Mark's Gospel. It points backward and forward in a variety of ways. It points backward to the activity of Moses on Mount Sinai:

> *Then Moses went up on the mountain, and the cloud covered the mountain. The glory of the Lord settled on Mount Sinai, and the cloud covered it six days; and on the seventh day he called to Moses out of the midst of the cloud (Ex 24:15–16).*

The transfiguration points backward as well to the activity of Elijah on Mount Horeb (1 Kgs 19:8–18). These two great figures of the Old Testament are both prominent in Mark's presentation of the Good News. Moses was the lawgiver and the first of the prophets; Elijah was the prophet who towered above all the other prophets. In the first half of Mark's Gospel we saw Jesus presented as one whose authority exceeded that of Moses. In the second half we will see Jesus presented as the prophet who will supersede Elijah as the one speaking God's word in the final hour.

Three times in Mark's Gospel Jesus takes his three closest disciples to be with him for his most intimate self-revelations (5:37; 9:2; 14:33). Three times in Mark's Gospel there is a Christophany, a non-demonic manifestation of Jesus as God's Son (1:11; 9:6; 15:39). This pivotal passage in the center of Mark's Gospel combines both of these crucial features.

The unfolding of Jesus' identity is nearing completion: he is the messiah, he is the lowly and majestic Son of Man, he is God's own Son. The first time Jesus was declared to be God's Son it was an announcement made to Jesus alone (1:11). Here it is announced to the three disciples (9:6). They hear the words but will not grasp their full meaning until Jesus is raised from the dead. The third and final Christophany is the only place where a human person understands who Jesus really is. There the centurion will declare: "This man was really the Son of God" (15:39).

In this Christophany Jesus has been transfigured before their eyes; his physical appearance has been changed to manifest the glorious presence of God's Kingdom (9:3). Moses and Elijah appear on the scene giving witness to the fulfillment of the Law and the prophets in Jesus (9:4). The Kingdom of God, however, is both already and not yet. Peter still cannot grasp the not yet character of the Kingdom and again misunderstands the revelation that is before his eyes.

> *Teacher, it is a good thing that we are here. We will make three tents, one for you, one for Moses, and one for Elijah (9:5).*

Scholastic theologians contrast time and eternity by saying that time is a now that changes while eternity is a now that stands still. When perfection is achieved there is no room or need for change; everything is the way it ought to be and remains forever that way. If this is hard to visualize, think of one of those rare moments of intense joy and happiness that we experience in our lives. In those moments we would like to be able to stop the clock and make the moment last forever.

With the appearance of Moses and Elijah Peter felt the final moment had arrived, that moment when God and his heavenly court would reside with man forever. Peter was satisfied with the already of the Kingdom. Jesus was indeed more than a political messiah; he was the Son of Man who had brought to completion the meeting of God and man. By setting up tents Peter intended to capture the moment and make it last forever.

In that moment of enthusiasm, joy and misunderstanding a cloud covered them and a voice declared:

> *This is my own dear Son—listen to him (9:7)!*

These words are very similar to the words spoken at the first
Christophany, Jesus' baptism:

> *You are my own dear Son. I am well pleased with you (1:11).*

The difference between them is that at the baptism Jesus is spoken to while at the transfiguration the disciples are spoken to.
They are told to listen to Jesus, for Jesus is not only the fulfillment of the Law but the fulfillment of the prophets as well. As
the perfection of all the prophets, beginning with Moses, reaching its peak in Elijah and ending with John, Jesus perfectly speaks
God's word.

The people think that Jesus is John, Elijah or a prophet. He is a
prophet, but not one of the prophets of old. Peter thinks Jesus is
the messiah. He is, but he is also the suffering Son of Man who
will come in glory to rule the world. Can one person be all these
things at the same time? The Son of God can. The voice from
heaven has focused on the real identity of Jesus which underlies
all of these correct but limited ways of thinking about him.

The three disciples, having heard the words, took a quick look
around and saw only Jesus (9:8). Moses and Elijah have vanished.
By their presence they witnessed the fulfillment of Law and
prophecy in Jesus. By their disappearance they testified that the
fullness of all God's promises is now to be found in Jesus and in
him alone.

The three disciples will show, by their subsequent behavior,
that they have not understood the meaning of this revelation.
Not until their personal faith experience of the resurrected Jesus
will its meaning become clear. For this reason Jesus orders them:

> *Don't tell anyone what you have seen, until the Son of Man has
> risen from death (9:9).*

Two important features emerge in this command. First, it is the
last time in Mark's Gospel that Jesus commands secrecy. Jesus
had prevented the demons from revealing his identity (1:25, 34;
3:11–12; 5:7). He had forbidden people to talk about his healing

miracles (1:44; 5:43; 7:36; 8:26), although they disobeyed this order. He had ordered the disciples not to discuss their opinion that
he was the messiah (8:30). Now, in his last command to secrecy,
he orders the three to keep silent about the revelation on the
mount of the transfiguration. This last time, however, he places a
limit on the secrecy: "until the Son of Man has risen from death"
(9:9). The reason for secrecy is the same in each case. A partial
understanding can lead to serious misunderstanding. Here, in the
last command to secrecy, we are told when full understanding
will be possible and the need for secrecy will cease.

The second noteworthy feature of this last command to secrecy
is that it is obeyed (9:10). Why they obey is not explained, but it
is perhaps true to say that they were simply incapable of talking
about a fantastic event that exceeded their comprehension. In any
event it is very significant for Mark that they obeyed. Because of
their silence the confession of the centurion at the foot of the
cross will clearly not be a repetition of words he has heard but a
genuine faith perception of the full reality of Jesus (15:39).

2. Discussion about Elijah, 9:10–13

The astounding revelations at the opening of the second half of
Mark's Gospel are brought to a conclusion with this discussion
about Elijah. The revelations began on the way to Caesarea Philippi when Jesus asked who people thought he was (8:27). The
revelations conclude on the way down the mountain with the
disciples still unclear about the relationship between Jesus and
Elijah. They ask Jesus:

Why do the teachers of the Law say that Elijah has to come first
(9:11)?

The reason why they ask this particular question is not entirely
clear but certainly involves their failure to understand the transfiguration and probably is a result of their thinking that the end
had already come.

According to 2 Kgs 2:11–12 Elijah did not die but instead was

carried up to heaven in a fiery chariot. According to the prophet
Malachi:

> Behold, I will send you Elijah the prophet before the great and
> terrible day of the Lord comes (Mal 4:5).

Elijah was expected as the forerunner of God's final judgment. If
the end has already come, however, why is it said that Elijah
must come first? The disciples' question envisions two possibili-
ties: either Elijah has come and the end has arrived or Elijah has
not yet come and the end is yet to arrive. Jesus, however, answers
with a third and unexpected alternative: Elijah has come but the
end has not yet arrived. Even more significant, however, is that
with this response Jesus is able to turn the discussion around to
the one point the disciples seem unable or unwilling to grasp, i.e.,
suffering. Jesus answers their question with a question:

> Why do the Scriptures say that the Son of Man will suffer much
> and be rejected (9:12)?

By juxtaposing the two questions Mark once again points to the
already and not yet nature of the Kingdom. Elijah has indeed
come, but suffering, rejection and death are necessary before all
will be accomplished. In the final verse of this passage Jesus goes
on to explain that Elijah (in the person of John the Baptist) is not
only the forerunner of the end time of the Kingdom but more importantly is the forerunner of the suffering, rejection and death of
the Son of Man (see 6:17–29).

D. EPILEPTIC DEMONIAC, 9:14–29

OVERVIEW. In the second half of Mark's Gospel there are only
two healing miracles: this one, located at the end of the material
following the first passion prediction, and the cure of the blind
man at Jericho (10:45–52), located at the end of the material following the third and final passion prediction. Unlike the miracles
of the first half which were of a more private nature, both of
these are performed before great crowds (9:14; 10:45), and no se-

crecy is demanded of anyone. Unlike the last two miracles of the first half, however, these two place great emphasis on faith (9:19, 23, 24; 10:52).

In the first of these we are presented with a boy possessed by an evil spirit who causes the boy to display the symptoms of epilepsy. For this reason the boy is often referred to as the epileptic demoniac. Mark has carefully constructed this story in three separate scenes. He uses the story to summarize and conclude the ideas developed in the sequence which began with the first passion prediction (8:31).

1. The Disciples' Inability, 9:14–19

In the presence of a great crowd Jesus is confronted not simply with a person to be healed but with a more complex problem, i.e., the inability of his disciples to heal. Jesus is stronger than Satan and has given to his disciples the authority to drive out evil spirits (6:7). Why, then, are they unable to drive out this evil spirit? The question will not be answered until the end of the passage (9:29) but in this first scene we are shown both the scope of the problem and the direction of the solution.

As the scene develops we see the disciples arguing with the teachers of the Law over their inability to cast out. The teachers of the Law have no role in the story other than their appearance at the beginning. They appear here merely to indicate that this problem is not just an isolated and individual case but rather a universal problem which involves the entire faith community as it confronts and conflicts with the enemies of faith.

The rebuke of Jesus at the end of this scene points out the direction of the solution:

> *How unbelieving you people are!*
> *How long must I stay with you?*
> *How long do I have to put up with you (9:19)?*

The lack of faith on the part of the disciples lies at the root of their inability. Their lack of faith is also the primary cause of the suffering which must occur before the fullness of the Kingdom arrives.

2. The Father's Faith, 9:19–24

At this point Jesus turns his attention away from the disciples and toward the father. As soon as the possessed boy is in the presence of Jesus the demon casts the boy into a fit. The opposition between the Kingdoms of God and Satan is heightened into a rage before the Kingdom of God is victorious.

Jesus discusses the boy's condition with the father who entreats Jesus:

Have pity on us and help us, if you possibly can (9:22)!

We are reminded here of the first time Jesus encountered a man with hesitant faith, the leper (1:40). In that story Jesus responded in pity to the hesitant faith (1:41). Here, however, Jesus uses the incident as an occasion to teach about the role and necessity of faith:

Everything is possible for the person who has faith (9:23).

In this discussion Jesus is preparing for the resolution of the problem about the disciples' inability. Here the father displays precisely that attitude which is lacking in the disciples:

I do have faith, but not enough. Help me have more (9:24)!

Genuine faith involves recognition of our own inadequacy and the concomitant recognition that we are totally dependent on God even for the faith by which we depend on him. To the extent that we trust in ourselves, to that extent we are lacking in faith. By acknowledging our weakness, however, we acknowledge that faith itself is a gift and that we are open to the action of God filling our need. The father has this genuine attitude of faith. Do the disciples?

3. Need for Prayer, 9:25–29

The third scene opens with the father disappearing from view and the crowd once again prominent. Jesus commands the evil

spirit to leave the boy with language that recalls the first casting
out of an evil spirit:

> *Be quiet, and come out of the man (1:25)!*
> *I order you to come out of the boy (9:25).*

The effect of the cure is described, as in previous miracles, in
terms that are deliberately chosen to make one think of Jesus' dying and rising (9:26–27). Here, however, the connection is more
graphic and explicit and clearly connects this miracle with the
passion prediction at the beginning of this section (8:31).

After the passion prediction and Peter's misunderstanding Jesus had instructed the crowd on the real meaning of discipleship
(8:34—9:1). After this parabolic act which explains the need for
Jesus' suffering as well as providing an example of true discipleship, the disciples still do not understand why they failed to drive
out the evil spirit (9:28). Jesus' response is a brief but complete
summary of this entire passion prediction sequence:

> *Only prayer can drive this kind out; nothing else can (9:29).*

Those who have forgotten themselves, borne the mark of their
commitment and followed Jesus (8:34) are the true disciples.
These are the ones who recognize that all power is found in God
and not in the heart and soul of the believer. These are the ones
who recognize that Christian discipleship is not for a time only
but forever. Prayer, then, is more than an act of faith; it is an act
of faith that recognizes its own inadequacy.

A contemporary spiritual writer, Henri Nouwen, has described
the spiritual life in terms of three movements (*Reaching Out,* Garden City, 1975). His third movement might roughly correspond to
the unitive way of the classical writers. This third movement is
the movement "from illusion to prayer," a movement away from
misconceptions about our own abilities and importance and toward a pure openness and receptivity to the action of God.

The disciples were unable to cast out the demon because of a
lack of the kind of faith that is required for prayer and the presence of an illusion of self-grandeur which is an obstacle to

prayer. The disciples thought they were independent, that they possessed the power to cast out demons.

In God's Kingdom, however, there is no independent human achievement. Even as persons of faith what we achieve is not the result of the effectiveness of our piety. It is God who gives success to our works. The disciples are presented here as already slipping into that positive misunderstanding that will place them at odds with God's Kingdom.

STUDY QUESTIONS

1. How do we picture Jesus? As the Messiah? As the suffering servant? As the coming Son of Man? Do we appreciate how difficult it was for Peter and the others to grasp the unity of these different ideas?

2. Do we ever try to make people measure up to our pre-conceived ideas about what they should be? Do we ever do this to the Church? Have we done this to Jesus (8:32)?

3. What does it mean to be a follower of Jesus? Have we ever experienced a call to surrender our lives? To carry our cross? Have we ever been ashamed of Jesus?

4. At the transfiguration the disciples experienced the presence of God. Have there ever been moments when we have been certain of the presence of God? Have we desired to stop the clock, or have we been filled with an enthusiasm to continue the work of God?

5. In doing God's work do we rely on our own strength? Can we see the failure of the disciples in our own church community (9:18)? Do we have the humility and the courage to pray as the boy's father did (9:24)?

Chapter Six

TRUE DISCIPLESHIP

SUMMARY. After showing us who Jesus really is, Mark now explains what it is to be a disciple of Jesus. In the previous chapter we saw Jesus predicting his passion and calling on the disciples to take up their cross and follow him. In this chapter we will consider the second and third passion predictions together with the teachings on discipleship that follow each of them. Christian discipleship, we will see, consists in a total reversal of values. It is better to be a child than an adult; it is better to be a servant than a master.

The disciples' continued misunderstanding highlights Mark's radical teaching on discipleship. In the end it is not a disciple but a blind man who realizes he is blind and cries out: "Son of David, have mercy on me" (10:47).

Have our commitments to the ways and values of this world left us blind to the reality of Christian discipleship? Can we cry out with the faith of the blind man: "Son of David, have mercy on me"?

READ 9:30–10:52

OVERVIEW. With the first passion prediction Mark opened up a whole new dimension of Jesus' identity, i.e., the suffering Son of

Man. Using the disciples' reaction and Jesus' subsequent words and deeds, Mark develops the notion of Christian discipleship. In the passages following the second and third passion predictions this notion of Christian discipleship becomes the primary focus.

Discipleship involves a fundamental reversal of values. "Whoever wants to save his life will lose it" (8:35). The final parabolic action following the first prediction depicted the disciples' clinging to their own identity and failing, while the father of the boy surrendered in faith to Jesus (9:14–29). This same reversal of values is intensified in the material which follows the second and third predictions. After the second the superiority of the child over the adult is emphasized; after the third it is the superiority of the servant over the master.

Throughout this section on the passion predictions there are geographical references which Mark has included for their theological significance. The first prediction occurs in the Gentile city of Caesarea Philippi, the second in Galilee and the third in Judea. After the first Jesus ascends a mountain, there receiving the approval of God. After the second he enters Judea, there receiving the disapproval of the Pharisees. After the third he heads for Jerusalem, there to die.

The entire section moves from the cure of the blind man at Bethsaida (8:22–26) to the cure of the blind man at Jericho (10:46–52). Mark is showing Jesus gradually revealing his own identity as he shows us what true discipleship is all about. The gradual healing at Bethsaida leads up to the immediate cure at Jericho where the man sees clearly and follows Jesus. The passages we are now reading should open our eyes and help us to follow Jesus.

A. CHILDREN ENTER THE KINGDOM, 9:30—10:31

1. Second Passion Prediction, 9:30–37

a. Prediction, 9:30–31

The second prediction begins with an indefinite geographical note:

> *They left that place and went on through Galilee (9:30).*

It is uncertain what "that place" was, as it is equally uncertain where in Galilee this event takes place. What is significant for Mark is that Jesus is resolutely moving toward his appointed destiny. From the outlying Gentile region of Caesarea Philippi where he first revealed that destiny he has moved south to Galilee, his native region and the region in which he carried on the greater part of his ministry. Here in Jewish territory he reaffirms his conviction that he must die.

The previous time when Jesus was in Galilee he had to contend with the misunderstandings and political aspirations of the people. On this journey through Galilee (9:30–49) he avoids the people entirely (9:30, 33). Not until he arrives in Judea (10:1) does anyone other than his disciples know of his presence. They are alone with him, somewhere in Galilee, when he says:

> *The Son of Man will be handed over to men who will kill him; three days later, however, he will rise to life (9:31).*

This prediction is briefer than the first (8:31) but contains one new feature: his death will come about as a result of his being handed over, i.e., he will be betrayed. There is no indication as yet concerning who will betray him or how, just as there is no indication concerning who will kill him or how. The events soon to take place are, however, slowly coming into focus.

b. Misunderstanding, 9:32–34

After the first passion prediction Peter began to rebuke Jesus (8:32). The disciples still do not understand what Jesus is talking about but this time they are afraid to say anything (9:32). They do, however, display their ignorance on the road to Capernaum. Had they understood Jesus' willingness to abandon himself to the will of men they would never have argued about who was the greatest.

It is natural and normal for a mature adult to look out for his own interests. Recklessly abandoning oneself to the interests or caprices of others is, in the eyes of the sensible, foolish. Yet somehow what Jesus is all about involves this reckless abandonment, this lack of concern for self. In Paul's words:

> *We proclaim Christ on the cross, a message that is offensive to the Jews and nonsense to the Gentiles; but for those whom God has called, both Jews and Gentiles, this message is Christ, who is the power of God and the Wisdom of God. For what seems to be God's foolishness is wiser than men's wisdom, and what seems to be God's weakness is stronger than men's strength (1 Cor 1:23–25).*

Somehow the disciples do not understand. Even worse, they positively misunderstand and move in the opposite direction. They are not only concerned with their own personal well being but are concerned about who among them is the greatest.

c. Instruction, 9:35–37

What is the nature of their misunderstanding? How is it to be corrected? The disciples' basic error was that they thought they were adults. An adult is someone who has emerged from adolescence into that autonomous, free existence in which one is responsible for one's own person and free to chart one's future course. This basic error began to emerge at the end of the previous sequence where the disciples thought their discipleship was a kind of adolescence that would yield to mature independence. They were amazed when their independent activity was unable to cast out the evil spirit (9:28). Now they are not only satisfied with their independence but are concerned over which of them is the greatest.

The image of the child is a magnificent image for correcting this misunderstanding. A child is not free to make its own decisions, to chart its own course in life, because it is not yet strong enough or wise enough or stable enough. A child is not capable of assuming responsibility for his own existence. He must depend on his parents and trust in them.

There are aspects of childhood that are desirable and others that are undesirable. A child is free from the concerns and anxieties of adult existence. A child need not worry about what he will eat, where he will live or how he will be clothed. A child is free from the burden of providing for his present needs as well as free from the anxiety of planning for the future. The freedom of a child is, however, very different from that adult freedom that every person yearns for as soon as the tensions of adolescence begin to be felt. Few, if any, would be willing to give up their adult freedom and return to the fragile, limited, dependent existence of a child.

Perhaps the most undesirable aspect of childhood is vulnerability. In the presence of the protection and support of loving parents the child can grow and develop into a mature adult. Apart from this protection and support the child is helpless and is an easy victim for any harmful force that comes along.

Jesus, in the second passion prediction, indicated that the Son of Man was vulnerable with the vulnerability of a child. Against one who would betray him he was defenseless. The disciples miss his point entirely. Their subsequent behavior indicates how distant man's ways are from God's ways.

In response to their quest for greatness Jesus says:

> *Whoever wants to be first must place himself last of all and be the servant of all (9:35).*

With these words he summarizes the total reversal of values which will be explained in the remainder of this section. These words point forward to the words Jesus will speak about himself just before his final cure, the healing of the blind man at Jericho.

> *Even the Son of Man did not come to be served; he came to serve and to give his life to redeem many people (10:45).*

In this first instruction, however, Jesus focuses on another aspect of this reversal of values. He places a child in front of them and identifies the family of God's Kingdom with the child:

> *Whoever in my name welcomes one of these children, welcomes me; and whoever welcomes me, welcomes not only me but also the one who sent me (9:37).*

Jesus is doing much more here than encouraging the disciples to be kind to children. He is extolling the weakness, vulnerability, openness, dependence and trust of a child. Precisely because a child is characterized by all of these things he is identified with Jesus and with the Father. Precisely because he is all of these things he resides in God's Kingdom. The disciples, Jesus implies, would be closer to God's Kingdom if they were more like children.

2. Further Instructions, 9:38—10:31

OVERVIEW. The disciples had misunderstood their role as followers of Jesus because they had failed to grasp who Jesus was. Mark now adds five passages which further develop that reversal of values expressed in the child image and bring out even more the true nature of Christian discipleship.

a. Anyone Can Be a Disciple, 9:38–41

Sociologists and psychologists tell us that the many kinds of prejudices that infect contemporary society are learned prejudices. Although adults are better able than children to conceal prejudices, children are marvelously free of them. Children are free of prejudices until their minds begin to be shaped by the hardened attitudes of those around them.

One of the most beautiful things about children is their unformed potential. They are not yet what they will be. They can still become almost anything. Children are full of promise, full of hope. Adults are often almost hopelessly bent out of shape by the hardening of their mature attitudes and ideas.

In this passage the disciples are again behaving like adults whose close-minded hostility has replaced the open-minded hospitality of a child. Convinced that they are correct and even great, they cannot conceive how someone different from themselves could be a disciple of Jesus. We are reminded here of Jesus' words earlier in the Gospel:

> *Whoever does what God wants him to do is my brother, my sister, my mother (3:35).*

Ultimately there are only two kingdoms, the Kingdom of God and the Kingdom of Satan. When Peter thought the thoughts of men Jesus rebuked him for being on the side of Satan (8:33). Here Jesus will insist that if one is not on the side of Satan he must be on the side of God.

Since dwelling in God's Kingdom involves being like a child, it involves as well the unformed potential of a child. True discipleship cannot be limited; it is open to an enormous variety of expression. The disciples reacted to a stranger like prejudiced adults:

> *We told him to stop, because he doesn't belong to our group (9:38).*

Jesus, however, insists that there are no pre-conceived limits to the expression of discipleship:

> *Whoever is not against us is for us (9:40).*

The final verse of this passage (9:41) is similar to the final verse in the preceding passage (9:37). Both carry meanings far more profound than first appears on the surface. The surface meaning is correct: anyone showing kindness to a Christian will be rewarded. Even more important, however, is the implication that "anyone" who does anything for Christ is himself a disciple.

b. Self-Denial, 9:42–50

This passage contains three loosely connected sayings about self-denial. The underlying concern in all of them is that self-affirmation excludes one from the Kingdom of God. Since self-affirmation results in spiritual death it would be advisable to go to any lengths to avoid it.

> [1] If anyone should cause one of these little ones to turn away from his faith in me, it would be better for that man to have a large millstone tied around his neck and be thrown into the sea (9:42).

This saying parallels the saying at the end of the previous passage (9:41). There anyone who did anything to help a believer was praised. Here anyone who does anything to hurt a believer is condemned. This saying is directed not at the Pharisees and others who have rejected Jesus and the Kingdom but at followers of Jesus who have misunderstood him and are leading others astray.

The true followers of Jesus are "these little ones" who recognize their limitations and their need for Jesus. Those who lead them astray are the followers of Jesus who think they can stand on their own, who think they understand the mysteries of the Kingdom. Paul had to deal with a similar situation at Corinth:

> *The person who thinks he knows something really doesn't know as he ought to know. But the man who loves God is known by him (1 Cor 8:2–3).*

Today Christians themselves constitute the greatest obstacle to the conversion of all mankind to the Gospel. The reason why so many people who hear the Good News do not turn and follow Jesus is because they see the lives of people who call themselves Christians, Christians whose affirmation of self is in effect a denial of Jesus and a stumbling block for the little ones just beginning to turn to Jesus.

> [2] If your hand makes you turn away, cut it off! It is better for you to enter life without a hand than to keep both hands and go off to hell. . . . (9:43–48).

This saying consists of three parallel sayings on hands, feet and eyes, followed by the words,

> *There their worms never die, and the fire is never put out (9:48).*

These last words are a quote from Is 66:24 and refer to a place called Gehenna, often used as an image of what hell must be like. Gehenna was a ravine south of Jerusalem that was used as a dump. Worms and parasites thrived there while fires were kept burning continuously to consume the rubbish.

These sayings are concrete and graphic restatements of the reversal of values called for in the initial teaching on discipleship:

> *Whoever wants to save his life will lose it (8:35).*

Here, however, Mark's concern is with self-denial and specifically as it relates to the image of the child. The danger with adults is that as they grow and mature they become set in their ways. They can become so protective of their wealth, so proud of their achievements, so jealous of their family and friends, so concerned about their beauty or health that a childlike attitude toward the Kingdom becomes impossible.

> *Does a man gain anything if he wins the whole world but loses his life (8:36)?*

A childlike attitude toward the Kingdom could demand a radical alteration in the set ways of our adult existence. The Good News of the Kingdom is becoming clearer. Do we still have ears to hear and eyes to see?

> [3] Everyone will be salted with fire. Salt is good; but if it loses its saltness, how can you make it salty again? Have salt in yourselves, and be at peace with one another (9:49–50).

Salt symbolizes the purification that a disciple must undergo, the changes that come over a person who leaves his former way of life to follow Jesus. Often there is considerable pain and suffering involved in the purifications we undergo, i.e., we are salted with fire. We know, however, that our new life with Jesus is worth whatever pain and suffering might be involved, i.e., salt is good.

The problem Jesus saw in his disciples was that they were losing the fervor of their first following of him. Their misunderstanding of the Good News was allowing their self-denial to turn to self-affirmation. They were losing their saltness.

Jesus encourages them to retain their attitude of dependency, their childlike attitude. As long as they retain their saltness there will be no place for pride, jealousy, greed, anger, etc. Disputes, like the one about greatness (9:34), will not occur and they will be at peace with one another.

c. The Problem of Divorce, 10:1–12

The New Testament teaching on divorce is not entirely clear. Each of the various passages that treat this subject has a different perspective (Mt 5:31–32; 19:3–9; Lk 16:18; Rom 7:2–3; 1 Cor 7:10–16). They do agree that Jesus was much more insistent on the permanency and indissolubility of marriage than were the teachers of the Law. What is most important for us, however, is not the precise details of Jesus' teaching on divorce but Mark's reason for including this story at this point in his Gospel.

Mark has taken a conflict story and presented it here as a parabolic incident further expanding his teaching on the childlikeness of discipleship. As with other parabolic teaching the disciples do not understand and have to have the matter explained to them in private (10:10–12). As with other parabolic teachings, however, the explanation fails to convey the full meaning of the parable (see 4:1–20).

The story opens with another indefinite geographical reference (10:1; see 9:30). What is significant here is that Jesus has left Galilee and is now approaching the very heart of Jewish territory. He has come, for the first time since his baptism, to Judea. The crowds that were absent as he travelled through Galilee are now seen again. Among them are Pharisees who try to trap Jesus (10:2).

Once before the Pharisees had tried to trap Jesus by seeking a sign (8:11). Now they try to trap him by having him acknowledge that Scripture can be twisted to man's advantage. In the second temptation in Matthew's Gospel Satan says:

> *If you are God's Son, throw yourself down to the ground; because the scripture says, "God will give orders to his angels about you; they will hold you up with their hands, so that not even your feet will be hurt on the stones" (Mt 4:6).*

Similarly here, the Pharisees try to trap Jesus by having him misinterpret the Scriptures, i.e., interpreting them as men would interpret them and not as God's Son would. Jesus, however, will not be tempted. Here, as in other conflict stories, Jesus goes beyond legalistic formulations and shows an intimate understanding of the ultimate will of God.

Jesus responds to the Pharisees first by showing that Scripture itself has something more profound to say than the legalistic passage they are quoting from Dt 24:1–4. That passage had allowed divorce under certain circumstances but closer to the real will of God are the two passages in Genesis which Jesus proceeds to quote (Mk 10:6–7; see Gn 1:27; 2:24). Second, Jesus goes beyond all formulations to be found in the Law and pronounces with authority the will of God for man:

> *What therefore God has joined together, let no man put asunder (10:9).*

If we have been alert to Mark's intention in this parabolic incident we would realize that the explanation offered in 10:10–12 does not do justice to the insight Jesus has offered us in 10:9. Mark has been teaching about discipleship, about self-denial, about following Jesus with a childlike trust. The tendency of most adults, once they have "learned the ropes," is to cut corners, to find the easy way, to turn situations to their advantage, in short, to affirm themselves. The problem of divorce is just one manifestation of this adult tendency to try to make things go our way rather than letting things go God's way.

The true disciple has turned and followed Jesus. The life of discipleship, the life of childlike trust, is, moreover, a life that God has accomplished in the disciple. For a true disciple there is no turning back.

d. The Kingdom Is for Children, 10:13–16

This passage gives explicit expression to the main idea that pervades all five of these passages. Three times in these passages Jesus uses the solemn affirmation formula, "Amen, I say to you" (9:41; 10:15; 10:29). The solemn affirmation in this passage brings out the very essence of discipleship:

> *Remember this! Whoever does not receive the Kingdom of God like a child will never enter it (10:15).*

In the previous passage we were given the example of the Pharisees as people who sought to have their own way and thus excluded themselves from God's Kingdom. They were presented as enemies of Jesus, as agents of Satan, who came to trap Jesus. In this passage it is the friends of Jesus, the disciples who are presented as letting their own ideas become obstacles to the Kingdom.

In the first passage of this series the disciples were upset when someone other than themselves was casting out demons in Jesus' name (9:38). Now they are upset when children are brought to Jesus (10:13). They probably felt that discipleship was meant for mature sensible people like themselves and that there was no need for Jesus to waste his time on children.

In the first passage Jesus responded with a solemn affirmation in which he declared that anyone could be a disciple (9:41). Here Jesus insists that even children can be disciples and, what is more, only those who adopt a childlike stance toward the Kingdom will enter it (10:15).

The story opens with people bringing children to Jesus to be touched by him (see 1:41; 3:10; 5:27, 41; 6:5, 56; 7:33; 8:22). Often the faith that was indicated by a desire to touch Jesus was a weak faith possibly tinged with magical notions. Jesus had had enough of this kind of misplaced enthusiasm in Galilee. Here in Judea the disciples felt they were only protecting him from further aggravation.

Jesus, however, has another perspective. He not only allows the children to come to him but he scolds the disciples. They have presumed to understand what discipleship is all about when, in fact, they are the prime examples of misunderstanding. The children afford Jesus an opportunity to correct the disciples' misunderstanding.

The teaching of this passage is accomplished in three steps. First, Jesus insists that the Kingdom belongs to children (10:14). Second, anyone who is not like a child cannot enter the Kingdom (10:15). Finally, he affirms both of these points by his actions. To show that the disciples were wrong in exluding children, he does what first had been asked of him—he touches each of them. To show that it is only children who may enter God's Kingdom, he blesses them. Jesus had blessed the bread at the miracle of the loaves as he will bless the bread at the Last Supper. Apart from this passage, however, there is no place in the Gospel where he blesses people. It is only children who are blessed, only children who may enter God's Kingdom.

e. The Difficulty for the Rich, 10:17–31

The final passage in this series is a parabolic incident presented here in three parts: the story of the rich man (10:17–22), Jesus' teaching (10:23–27), and application to the disciples (10:28–31).

The passage is designed by Mark to complete the teaching on the childlikeness of the true disciple. The previous passage was about those included in the Kingdom. This passage is about those excluded.

The story opens with a man coming to Jesus and asking for entrance into the Kingdom. The dialogue that follows serves to show the genuineness of the man's faith. Satisfied that he is truly open to the Good News of the Kingdom Jesus informs him about what is required of a disciple. His words are similar to those spoken after the first passion prediction:

> *If anyone wants to come with me, he must forget himself, carry his cross, and follow me (8:34).*

> *Go and sell all you have and give the money to the poor, and you will have riches in heaven; then come and follow me (10:21).*

The childlikeness required for the Kingdom involves a kind of self-denial that is different for each person. For each person, however, the call to let go strikes at what is most difficult.

The man was very rich, and in spite of his initial faith he was unable to let go. Instead he went away sad (10:22).

When Jesus is alone with his disciples he teaches them the meaning of the incident:

> *It is much harder for a rich man to enter the Kingdom of God than for a camel to go through the eye of a needle (10:24).*

The man who prompted this saying was rich in material goods, but everyone is rich in things that can serve as obstacles to God's Kingdom. If it is hard for the materially wealthy it is hard as well for those who are intelligent or handsome or strong or popular or proud or lustful or covetous or cruel. Whatever is important in our lives can serve to cut us off from God's Kingdom.

The Good News is that the time has come when everything can be the way God wants it to be. As Mark unfolds for us this Good News we see that the requirements of the Kingdom are so severe that the Good News is beginning to sound like bad news. The disciples respond to this hard teaching by raising the question:

Who, then, can be saved (10:26)?

Jesus' response shows that the Good News is Good News indeed:

This is impossible for men, but not for God; everything is possible for God (10:27).

In the final passage following the first passion prediction Jesus had said to the father of the epileptic demoniac:

Everything is possible for the person who has faith (9:23).

Here, in the final passage following the second passion prediction Jesus maintains that even the childlike faith which seems impossible for men is possible for God. The Good News consists essentially in this: that what we are incapable of, i.e., forgetting ourselves and following Jesus, God is capable of and will do for us if we let him.

The passage ends with Peter once again jumping to conclusions as he had done at Caesarea Philippi. There he thought he knew who Jesus was but soon was proven to have been mistaken. Here he thinks he knows what discipleship is:

Look, we have left everything and followed you (10:28).

He will repeat this commitment to discipleship at the Last Supper:

I will never leave you, even though all the rest do (14:29).

Shortly afterward, in the courtyard of the high priest he will deny Jesus three times (14:66–72).

Rather than criticize Peter, however, for his overzealous enthu-

siasm, Jesus restates the truth that Peter has grasped in the third
solemn affirmation in this series of passages:

> *I tell you this: anyone who leaves home or sisters or mother or
> father or children or fields for me, and for the gospel, will receive
> much more in this present age. He will receive a hundred times
> more houses, brothers, sisters, mothers, children, and fields—and
> persecutions as well; and in the age to come he will receive eternal
> life (10:29–30).*

A true disciple is one who has forgotten himself and become a
child in the Kingdom, one who has left everything and anything
that could separate him from God in Jesus. A true disciple, however, like a child will be cared for far more abundantly than he
could care for himself. Although he will be called upon to suffer
for the sake of Jesus and the Gospel, nothing that he truly needs
will be denied him, and he already possesses the promise of eternal life.

The passage ends with a cryptic affirmation of the consequences of that reversal of values that is demanded of the disciple
and is imaged in the child.

> *Many who now are first will be last, and many who now are
> last will be first (10:31).*

B. DISCIPLESHIP IS SERVICE, 10:32–52

OVERVIEW. About a thousand years before Jesus, King David
conquered the Jebusite city of Jerusalem and made it his capital.
Since that time the city of David, as it was called, had been the
political and religious center of Jewish life. Jesus is now on the
road to Jerusalem (10:32). In the final passage in this section
(10:46–52) he will be addressed as "Son of David" for the first
and only time in Mark's Gospel.

The questions about the identity of Jesus and what it means to
be his disciple continue to be raised. Almost within sight of Jerusalem the kingly nature of his person and mission begins to be
felt ever more strongly by those who are with him. Jesus, howev-

er, will attempt to show his followers that both messiahship and discipleship consist in service.

1. Third Passion Prediction, 10:32–45

a. Prediction, 10:32–34

A number of features distinguish this third and final passion prediction from the other two. At the time of the first prediction Jesus is alone with his disciples at Caesarea Philippi while at the second he is alone with them in Galilee. At the time of the third, however, Jesus is in Judea headed for Jerusalem, followed not only by the disciples but also by a crowd of people as well. The disciples were alarmed and the people afraid (10:32). Why? Probably because Jesus was going *to* Jerusalem!

This mention of Jerusalem is only the fifth that has occurred in Mark's Gospel, and all of the previous occurrences spoke of people coming *from* Jerusalem. We were told in the beginning that people came from Jerusalem to hear John (1:5). Then we saw people coming from Jerusalem three times to see Jesus in Galilee (3:8, 22; 7:1). Nowhere were we told that Jesus even planned to go to Jerusalem. Many of his followers hoped he would go there to assume the throne of David. Even these, however, with the first sight of Jesus actually moving toward the city, were filled with alarm and fear.

Even though a crowd is present the actual prediction is again reserved for the twelve (10:32). This prediction, unlike the others, begins with the word "Listen" (10:33). The disciples had misunderstood the first two predictions; now, in this third and final announcement, Jesus is emphasizing the need to comprehend.

The first part of the prediction is entirely new: "We are going up to Jerusalem" (10:32). The disciples had already observed that they were headed for the city of David, but now Jesus explains why they are going there. It is in Jerusalem that he will suffer and die as he had predicted.

This prediction repeats and combines features from the first two predictions. In the first we were told that he would be rejected by the Sanhedrin and then put to death (8:31). In the second we were told that he would be handed over to men who would kill him (9:31). In this prediction we hear that he will be handed over to the Sanhedrin who will condemn but not kill him. They in turn will hand him over to Gentiles who will abuse and then kill him.

This prediction is the fullest explanation yet about what will happen, but we are still uninformed about who will betray him and also about how he will be executed.

b. James and John Misunderstand, 10:35–40

After the first prediction it was Peter who misunderstood; now it is the other two of the three most favored disciples. Like Peter before them they are filled with expectations of the reign of a political messiah. As they approach Jerusalem they fail to hear the words Jesus speaks in his final passion prediction. Instead their misunderstanding leads them into a personal lust for power. They are like politicians who start maneuvering for cabinet positions as soon as it appears likely that their candidate will win.

Jesus responds to their request for seats at his right and left (10:37) with a question of his own:

> *Can you drink the cup that I must drink? Can you be baptized in the way I must be baptized (10:38)?*

They insist that they can (10:39), still not realizing what Jesus is talking about. The cup he will drink is his suffering about which he will pray in the garden of Gethsemane:

> *Take this cup away from me. But not what I want, but what you want (14:36).*

Sacramental baptism is a symbolic dying to the forces of evil and rising to new life in God's Kingdom. Jesus' baptism was real. He really suffered and died in the final combat with the forces of evil and really rose to new life in God's Kingdom so that we might be able to share in his victory and his life.

Jesus responds to James and John, as he had just responded to Peter (10:29–31), with understanding and benevolence, for he knows that soon their eyes will be opened. After he has risen they will see the full reality of the Good News and, responding to the grace of God, will fulfill their mission in God's Kingdom.

c. Instruction, 10:41–45

When the other ten heard about the request of James and John they were angry. They were angry not because James and John had misunderstood Jesus but because they were trying to establish themselves as superior to the rest. Jesus responds to all twelve with a third teaching on the reversal of values:

[1] Whoever wants to save his own life will lose it. . . . (8:35).

[2] Whoever does not receive the Kingdom of God like a child will never enter it (10:15).

[3] If one of you wants to be great, he must be the servant of the rest; and if one of you wants to be first, he must be the slave of all (10:43–44).

We have seen from the beginning of the Gospel that life in God's Kingdom has involved service to others (see Simon's mother-in-law, 1:31). Now, for the first time, Jesus teaches that service is not only something that happens in God's Kingdom, but is also an essential aspect of God's Kingdom. Service can take a wide variety of forms but its full Christian expression involves those forms of service which enable others to live in God's Kingdom.

The perfect expression of service in God's Kingdom is found in Jesus. Here he offers, for the first time, the ultimate reason why he must suffer and die. We learned early in the Gospel that Jesus' enemies intended to kill him (3:6). We learned through the passion predictions that his death was not simply the result of hostility but was necessarily involved in the fulfillment of his mission (8:31; 9:31; 10:33–34). Now we learn precisely how death is involved in the fulfillment of his mission:

> *For even the Son of Man did not come to be served; he came to serve and to give his life to redeem many people (10:45).*

For Jesus, death is an act of service for the rest of mankind, a service that will enable all to enter and live in God's Kingdom.

2. Blind Bartimaeus, 10:46–52

The section on the passion predictions concludes, as did the previous section, with the cure of a blind man. There Jesus gradually opened the eyes of the man at Bethsaida, showing that he was gradually opening the eyes of his disciples (8:22–26). Here at Jericho Jesus cures the blind man instantly. The time for gradual unfolding is over. Jesus is ready to enter Jerusalem where the full reality of who he is and what the Good News is all about will be painfully clear to all.

As with Peter at the beginning of this section (8:29) Jesus is recognized as the messiah. Here, however, Jesus is addressed as "Son of David," indicating the growing sentiment that Jesus was about to claim his throne in David's city. The person who addresses him is not even a follower of Jesus. He is simply a person on the side of the road caught up in the enthusiasm for Jesus. Most significantly, however, the man who calls out to Jesus is blind. He is blind both really and symbolically, for he too is filled with misconceptions about a political messiah.

Jesus asks the blind man the identical question he had asked James and John:

What do you want me to do for you (10:51; see 10:36)?

The response of the blind man, however, was far superior to that of James and John. They were filled with their own importance and wanted high positions in Jesus' government. The blind man, however, recognized his blindness and simply asked to be able to see.

Jesus grants his request, both really and symbolically. The initial faith that led the man to cry out for mercy is strengthened. He sees more fully who Jesus is. He follows Jesus, knowing perhaps better than any of the disciples where this following will bring him.

STUDY QUESTIONS

1. We are all children in God's Kingdom. Would we rather be adults? Do we try to be adults? What effect would a genuine desire on the part of everyone to be last of all (9:35) have on our local community?

2. How would Jesus react to the present-day scandal of a divided Christianity? Does 9:38–41 teach us anything about ecumenism?

3. Can we recall an earlier time in our life when we were on fire with zeal for living our discipleship? Are we losing that zeal (9:49–50)? How can we regain that zeal?

4. Is it possible to formulate minimum obligations for Christian living? Are such formulations really defining how much we can get away with? How should the Church today handle the problem of divorce and annulment?

5. In what ways are we rich? Are our riches an obstacle to our discipleship? Have we really left everything to follow Jesus (10:28)?

6. Bartimaeus knew he was blind (10:51); James and John did not (10:37). What do we want Jesus to do for us?

Chapter Seven

CONCLUSION OF PUBLIC MINISTRY

As the story of the Good News moves toward its climax we see two opposite developments. As the identity of Jesus becomes increasingly clear we see him being true to his identity and courageously fulfilling his mission. At the same time the disciples are less than anxious to accept the consequences of their discipleship.

We have followed Jesus through Galilee and Gentile lands and finally into Judea. In this chapter we will see him conclude his ministry with a solemn threefold entrance into Jerusalem. As he enters that city to meet his death he summarizes his teaching on the Good News of salvation: its compatibility with the Judaism of his day, the perfect realization of the will of God, the demands of faith, the nature of discipleship.

The teachings of this chapter are perhaps the most difficult in all of Mark's Gospel. Let us pray that the Spirit who guided Mark will help us appreciate and live the message of this section.

READ 11:1–13:37

OVERVIEW. The final section of Mark's Gospel before the climactic events of Jesus' passion, death and resurrection consists of three parts: first, Jesus' entrance into Jerusalem which is accomplished on three successive days and ends with the Jewish leaders' decision to arrest him (11:1—12:12); second, Jesus' final public teaching on the nature of God's Kingdom and true discipleship (12:13–44); finally, Jesus' farewell discourse to his disciples, often called the apocalyptic discourse (13:1–37).

This section (11:1–13:37) complements the previous section (8:27—10:52) which consisted of the three passion predictions together with the misunderstandings and instructions following each of them. There Jesus taught about his own destiny and what it meant for understanding the nature of discipleship. Here Jesus goes forth to meet his destiny and on the eve of his passion details the destiny that awaits his followers.

These two sections taken together (8:26—13:37) contain Mark's teaching on the nature of the Son of Man and its meaning for us. They are framed by two passages (8:31—9:1; 13:24–37) which set forth, in vivid detail, restatements of the initial proclamation of the Good News:

> *The right time has come and the Kingdom of God is near! Turn away from your sins and believe the Good News (1:15)!*

At the beginning of the second half of the Gospel the urgency for repentance and faith was expressed by the teaching on the suffering Son of Man (8:31) followed by the call to discipleship (8:34–37) and climaxed by the image of the glorious Son of Man who will judge man's fidelity (8:38—9:1). Our present section concludes in a similar way with an urgent call to watchfulness in the time between the suffering of the Son of Man and his final return (13:24–37).

A. ENTRANCE INTO JERUSALEM, 11:1—12:12

1. First Day—Triumphant Entry, 11:1–11

At long last Jesus has arrived at the outskirts of Jerusalem. The final days of his earthly life consist of two three-day periods, each of which begins in a similar fashion. At the beginning of both periods we find Jesus at Bethany, a town on the opposite side of the Mount of Olives, about a mile and a half from Jerusalem (11:1; 14:3). On both occasions he sends two disciples on ahead to make preparations (11:1–6; 14:13–16). Here he sends them to get a colt on which no one had ridden (11:2).

Jesus is about to enter Jerusalem for the first time in Mark's Gospel, an event which had been anticipated with fear and alarm by those who looked on him as a political messiah (10:32). However, this story unfolds in a way that attempts to correct all such messianic enthusiasm. First, the manner of entry is designed to emphasize the lowly aspect of the Son of Man. There seems to be a deliberate allusion to the prophet Zechariah:

> *Lo, your king comes to you; triumphant and victorious is he, humble and riding on an ass, on a colt the foal of an ass (Zech 9:9).*

It is significant as well that the colt had never been used (11:2), for such was the requirement for any animal used for a specifically religious purpose (Nm 19:2; Dt 21:3; 1 Sm 6:7). Jesus is entering Jerusalem not in majesty for a political purpose but in humility for a religious purpose.

Second, the response of the people along the way is wildly enthusiastic but also manifests a realization that Jesus is not simply a claimant to the throne of David. They spread their cloaks before him as people had done for Jehu when he seized the throne of Israel (1 Kgs 9:13), but they also spread branches before him, a specifically religious act associated with the feast of tabernacles (Ps 118:26–27). Their shouts are shouts of praise to God (11:9), and even though they look forward to the kingdom of David they do not refer to Jesus as David's son (11:10).

Finally, however, whatever messianic enthusiasm may have been present earlier in the day is no longer present as the incident draws to an end. When they arrive in Jerusalem the wildly cheering crowd is no longer evident. Perhaps they realized that Jesus was not going to claim the throne and lost interest in him. In any event Jesus enters the temple almost like a solitary tourist. He simply looks around and then returns to Bethany with the twelve (11:11).

2. Second Day, 11:12–19

a. Curse of the Fig Tree, 11:12–14

Jesus' threefold entrance into Jerusalem is designed by Mark to dramatize the transition from God's preparatory dealings with one people to God's Kingdom open to all peoples. The central event in these three days is the cleansing of the temple which takes place on the second day (11:15–19). To emphasize the importance of this event Mark again uses the technique of intercalation (see 3:20), framing this event with another symbolic act, the cursing of the fig tree.

The fig tree was often used in the Old Testament as a symbol for God's people (Jer 8:13; Hos 9:10; Jl 1:7). In this parabolic action Jesus sees a fig tree covered with leaves. Its outward appearance is inviting. However, when he goes to take some of its fruit, he finds none. God's chosen people, whom God had planted and nourished, do not show the fruit of God's benevolence to them when Jesus comes.

A failure to bear fruit indicates that something is radically wrong with the tree. When the grace of God fails to bear fruit in our lives it is because we have somehow created a blockage to the flow of that grace. Israel, in its leaders, had chosen not to respond to the coming of God's Kingdom among them. Because of this failure Jesus pronounced his curse:

No one shall ever eat figs from you again (11:14)!

A curious aspect of this story is the comment "because it was not the right time for figs" (11:13). If the tree could not have been expected to have any figs on it, why should it have been cursed? Lest this question prove troublesome there are two important considerations to bear in mind. First, Mark has taken various stories and sayings from the life of Jesus and arranged them in this three-day sequence. During the days just before Passover it was not the season for figs, but exactly when during the life of Jesus this symbolic act would have been performed we do not know.

The second consideration, however, is perhaps more important.

With this incident as well as with all the incidents and teachings of Mark's Gospel we must not be too insistent in imposing our modern logical approach on the Gospel narrative. Such an insistence could cause us to miss the real point of what Mark is doing. Symbolic acts are meant to arrest the attention and tease the mind beyond surface appearances. If we get too wrapped up in surface appearances we will never get to the main point which lies beyond.

b. Cleansing of the Temple, 11:15–19

Much of this section on Jesus' entrance into Jerusalem is rooted in imagery and words from the final part of the book of Zechariah, e.g., the lowly king riding on an ass (Zech 9:9). The final chapter of Zechariah speaks of the Day of the Lord when everything will be brought to completion. The last words of this chapter are:

> *There shall no longer be a trader in the house of the Lord of hosts on that day (Zech 14:21).*

Here, then, we have another symbolic act performed by Jesus, acting out the words of prophets and symbolically passing judgment on the Judaism of his day.

What exactly Jesus did we cannot be certain. The temple proper was of limited size, but the outer court was a vast area where all kinds of commercial operations took place. Records show that one merchant once had three thousand sheep for sale there. Whatever Jesus did, it was a prophetic, symbolic act that angered the leaders of the Jews. Two prophets are quoted by Jesus in explaining his act:

> *My house shall be called a house of prayer for all peoples (Is 56:7).*

> *Has this house, which is called by my name, become a den of robbers in your eyes (Jer 7:11)?*

Jesus drove the merchants out of the temple, but not simply because they were engaged in commercial operations. Such activity was quite normal in an area where people were required to make specific offerings, e.g., Joseph and Mary:

> *They also went to offer a sacrifice of a pair of doves or two young pigeons, as required by the law of the Lord (Lk 2:24).*

Jesus, in driving out the merchants, was symbolizing the end of the temple as the exclusive meeting place of God and man. Those who controlled the temple had used it for the their own glory and had closed their minds and hearts to any real contact with God. Jesus now declares by his act that from now on real contact with God will come about apart from the temple. No longer will there be any need to offer sacrifice and hence to buy and sell in the temple.

Jesus' quotation from Jeremiah is spoken in condemnation of the Jewish leaders. His quotation from Isaiah, however, reflects Mark's concern for universalism. Contact with God will now be available "for all people" (11:17).

The chief priests and teachers of the Law heard about Jesus' behavior. They must have understood the broader significance of what he had done. Their decision to kill him indicates that he represented, for them, much more than a reckless vandal who had disrupted legitimate temple activity.

Earlier, in Galilee, the Pharisees and Herodians, unlikely bedfellows, joined in planning to kill Jesus (3:6). They saw him as a threat to the authority they exercised over the people (see 8:15). Though they were mutual rivals, Jesus was a much greater threat and had to be eliminated.

Jesus will die, but not at the hands of the Pharisees and Herodians. He will not die as a result of his attempt to seize earthly power and authority. He will die as a result of being true to his own identity as Son of God. He will die as a result of his commitment to live and proclaim the reality of God's Kingdom among men.

Jesus' entrance into Jerusalem and the temple brings to a head the irreconcilable opposition between Judaism and the Kingdom of God. The leaders of the Jews recognize the ultimate threat he poses for their way of life. As his commitment to God's Kingdom becomes ever more clear, their decisions to kill him will only intensify and will soon succeed.

3. Third Day, 11:20—12:12

OVERVIEW. The third day of Jesus' ministry in Jerusalem actually extends from 11:20 to 13:37 and includes all of the teaching activity in the temple recorded by Mark. This compression of all of Jesus' activity into one day is, however, due to Mark's placing the three days of entrance immediately before the three days of suffering.

The material which Mark includes on the third day can, however, be divided into three parts, the first of which, 11:20—12:12, completes the cycle of entrance and confrontation. Jesus' final entrance into Jerusalem is preceded by an explanation of the fig tree. Upon his entrance into the temple Jesus is openly confronted by the Jewish leaders. He refuses to deal with them on their level but instead speaks his final parable. The leaders understand this parable well enough to solidify their determination to arrest Jesus.

a. Fig Tree, Faith and Prayer, 11:20–25

On the third day, as they walked along, "Peter remembered" (11:21). This comment might seem unimportant at first, but it shows a significant development from the situation at the end of the first half of the Gospel where Jesus rebuked the disciples with the words:

> *You have eyes—can't you see?*
> *You have ears—can't you hear?*
> *Don't you remember (8:18)?*

Peter remembered what Jesus had said to the fig tree. He understood its meaning. The fig tree is now dead (11:21); the temple can no longer claim to be the dispenser of the gifts of God. Now that there is no temple there is only faith (11:22). Now God is available not merely to those who can gain access to the temple but to all who have ears to hear and eyes to see.

Jesus explains the new situation with another of his solemn affirmations:

> *(Amen, I say to you) you can say to this hill, "Get up and*
> *throw yourself into the sea." If you do not doubt in your heart,*
> *but believe that what you say will happen, it will be done for you*
> *(11:23).*

Jesus' statement is, in a sense, an exaggeration, for no one has ever moved a mountain by faith. In a sense, however, it is literally true, for no one who has truly staked his life on Jesus would ever be denied anything he truly needs. It is highly unlikely, however, that anyone would need to have a mountain moved and equally unlikely that such a request could be the object of genuine prayer.

The kind of faith capable of moving mountains (1 Cor 13:2) is present only where there is a genuine attitude of prayer (11:24; see 9:29). When one recognizes completely one's inadequacy and relies totally on God even for an awareness of what it is one truly needs, then one can be certain that prayers will always be answered. Unlike Matthew and Luke, Mark nowhere records the Lord's Prayer (Mt 6:9–13; Lk 11:2–4). In this passage, however, he treats the main ideas of that prayer and concludes with the concern for forgiveness found in the Lord's Prayer (11:25).

b. Authority of Jesus, 11:27–33

The attitude of prayer which Jesus encourages is diametrically opposed to the attitude found in the Jewish leaders. They know what they have and what they need. They are not about to tolerate anyone who challenges them. At the end of the first half of Mark's Gospel the Pharisees

> *asked him to perform a miracle to show God's approval (8:11).*

Now the chief priests, the teachers of the Law and the elders (see 8:31) come to Jesus and ask:

> *What right do you have to do these things? Who gave you the right to do them (11:28)?*

Just as Jesus had earlier refused to work a miracle, so now he refuses to answer their question. Now, however, he does more than answer their question. He shows them why they are wrong in asking the question: first, with the example of John the Baptist, and, second, with the parable of the tenants.

Precisely because they are a fig tree that does not bear fruit, precisely because they are satisfied with themselves and refuse to be challenged with the word of God, precisely for these reasons they rejected John. They are rejecting Jesus for the same reasons. Jesus' response continues the parallel Mark is drawing between the fate of John and the fate of Jesus (see 6:17–29; 9:12–13).

c. Tenants in the Vineyard, 12:1–12

In the first half of the Gospel Mark showed Jesus unfolding the Good News with parabolic words and deeds. In the second half the reality of Jesus and the Kingdom begins to be clarified. After the cure of Bartimaeus (10:46–52) Jesus goes up to Jerusalem and no longer hides in secrecy his message or his destiny. The parable of the tenants, then, is not a parable in the strict sense which teases the mind of the believer into a fuller realization of the reality of God's Kingdom. It is instead an allegory on Jesus' place in the religious history of Israel, an allegory which even the obstinate enemies of Jesus can understand.

The story begins using the image of the vineyard which appeared in Is 5:1–7. The story itself is sufficiently true to life. It was customary in Palestine at that time for owners to lease their land to tenants in exchange for a percentage of the harvest. It would not be unheard of for tenants to withhold payment if they thought they could. Even the detail about murdering the son is plausible, for if an owner died without an heir the tenants could claim the vineyard.

The meaning of the allegory is obvious when one realizes that the owner is God, the tenants are the Jewish leaders, the servants are the prophets, and the son is Jesus. God, through the prophets, constantly called upon his people to show in their lives the fruit of their special relationship with him. This was the point of the story of the vineyard in the prophet Isaiah:

> *The vineyard of the Lord of hosts is the house of Israel, and the men of Judah are his pleasant planting; and he looked for justice, but behold, bloodshed; for righteousness but behold, a cry (Is 5:7)!*

Throughout their history the leaders of Israel and Judah treated the prophets shamefully (1 Kgs 22:27; Jer 37:15; 2 Chr 24:21; 36:15–16; Neh 9:26), ignoring them, insulting them, punishing them and even killing them.

The Jewish leaders of Jesus' day knew full well what he was talking about. Their hearts were so hardened, however, that they could not hear the real message of God's Kingdom; they only heard their condemnation and were enraged.

Mark added to the story of the vineyard the saying about the cornerstone in order to balance a story about death with a story about resurrection. The son may be rejected and killed but the result will not be reward for the tenants. They will be utterly destroyed, while a totally new reality will emerge founded on the stone that was rejected.

Jesus' third entrance into Jerusalem is completed in a manner similar to his second. There the leaders of the Jews "began looking for some way to kill Jesus" (11:18). Here they "tried to arrest Jesus" (12:12). They were unable to arrest him, however, because of his popularity with the crowd. They will wait for a more opportune time.

B. FINAL PUBLIC TEACHINGS, 12:13–44

OVERVIEW. These final teachings of Jesus consist of six passages, the first three being responses to questions asked of Jesus, the last three being teachings in which Jesus takes the initiative. The six together constitute a final effort on Jesus' part to communicate to all the people the full reality of God's Kingdom.

In these passages there is a procession of people: Pharisees, Herodians, Sadducees, teachers of the Law, the crowds. In Mark's compressed chronology all of these incidents happen on the third day. They probably are, however, among the incidents Jesus will refer to at his trial when he says, "Day after day I was with you teaching in the temple" (14:49).

1. Three Questions Asked of Jesus, 12:13–34

a. Paying Taxes, 12:13–17

The first characters we meet are the Pharisees and Herodians. They last appeared together back in 3:6 when they decided to kill Jesus. The desire to kill him has now shifted to the Jewish leaders, but the concern of the Pharisees and Herodians remains the same as it was earlier: power and authority.

For the third and final time the Pharisees try to trap Jesus (see 8:11; 10:2). As with the earlier incidents this third attempt is comparable to the third temptation by Satan in Matthew's Gospel. The responses of Jesus there and here are almost the same:

Worship the Lord your God and serve only him (Mt 4:10).

Pay to God what belongs to God (Mk 12:17).

Here in Mark the Pharisees and Herodians ask Jesus whether it is against their Law to pay taxes to the Roman emperor (12:14). Ever since direct Roman rule was established over Samaria, Judea and Idumea (in 6 A.D.) the inhabitants of these areas had to pay a poll tax with Roman coinage. The problem for the Pharisees was that Roman coins had the emperor's image on them, and Jewish law forbade the use of any kind of images. To pay the tax would violate Jewish law by using images. To refuse to pay would be an act of rebellion against Rome. What would Jesus do?

Pay to the Emperor what belongs to him, and pay to God what belongs to God (12:17).

The Pharisees are still caught up in superficial legalism. Jesus once again emphasizes the need to get beyond superficialities and make contact with the will of God. This saying is often read as indicating the proper relationship that ought to exist between church and state. It is really much more. Seen in the context of the preoccupation of the Pharisees and Herodians it is an urgent appeal to recognize that the demands of God's Kingdom totally transcend all other requirements. The demands of God's Kingdom are on a different level, a transcendent level; they point to a whole new reality.

b. Rising from the Dead, 12:18–27

The second passage contains another conflict pronouncement story, this one involving the Sadducees, a sect which appears nowhere else in Mark's Gospel. Their role here is simply to set the scene for the pronouncement which comes at the end of this passage:

He is the God of the living, not of the dead (12:27).

The Sadducees were the conservatives of Jewish religion. The Pharisees lived not only by the Law of Moses but also by the teachings of the ancestors and countless other traditions and observances of their own making. The Sadducees, on the other hand, accepted only the Law of Moses, rejecting any and all later developments. Belief in the resurrection of the dead is one of these later developments. It appears nowhere in the Law of Moses and only makes its first appearance in the Book of Daniel written around the year 165 B.C. (Dn 12:2).

The Sadducees challenge the concept of rising from death by constructing a hypothetical case based on the law of levirate marriage found in Dt 25:5–6. They, like the Pharisees and Herodians before them, raise a problem that seems to have no acceptable solution. If there is a resurrection and if a woman can have seven successive husbands, whose wife will she be in the resurrection?

Jesus responds, as he had done before, not by answering their questions, but by raising the discussion to a higher plane. His response is not so much an answer to their question as an explanation of why they are wrong in asking the question. First, since the resurrected life is totally different from our earthly life (see 1 Cor 15:35–50), it cannot be discussed in terms of earthly situations, e.g., marriages. Second, and more important, God's power is unlimited. What might seem impossible or absurd by our standards is possible with God (see 10:27). Proclaiming the power of the living God is the real purpose of the strange way Jesus explains the words of God to Moses (Dt 6:4).

The Sadducees worshipped the God of the dead, the God whose relationships with man are confined to the written words of the Law. Jesus proclaims the God of the living, a God who is alive to every situation that can arise in human affairs, a God whose power is sufficient for every imaginable need, a God who invites us to live the life of his Kingdom.

c. The Great Commandment, 12:28–24

This third passage is unique among the pronouncement stories in Mark. Here we have a dialogue in which Jesus agrees with and praises the attitude of the one questioning him. The first of these temple incidents focused on the necessity of our doing the will of God, the second on God's power to raise our life to a level beyond what we now experience. This third incident gives us an example of a person who is open to the will of God and manifests the transcending power of God in his understanding of God's will.

As in the first two passages a person, here a teacher of the Law, raises a difficult to answer question. As in the other passages Jesus does not give a simple answer. Here, asked for the most important commandment, Jesus responds by offering two different commandments from two different books of the Old Testament:

[1] Listen, Israel! The Lord our God is the only Lord. You must love the Lord your God with all your heart, with all your soul, with all your mind, and with all your strength (12:29–30, from Dt 6:5).

[2] You must love your fellow-man as yourself (12:31, from Lv 19:18).

The main point of this passage, however, emerges when the teacher of the Law restates the answer Jesus has given, a restatement that shows a profound understanding about God's dealings with men:

[1] Only the Lord is God, and that there is no other god but him (12:32).

[2] Man must love God with all his heart, and with all his mind and with all his strength; and he must love his fellow-man as himself (12:33).

The first statement corresponds to the pronouncement of Jesus in the first passage: "Pay to God what belongs to God" (12:17), while the second corresponds to the second pronouncement: "He is the God of the living, not of the dead" (12:27).

Only a religion based on dead laws could separate the love of God and the love of man. In a living, vibrant relationship with God the love of God is the love of one's fellow humans. Love is an openness to the reality of other people. The love which characterizes the Kingdom of God is a perfect openness to the will of God, an openness which embraces not only God but all God's people as well.

Because the teacher of the Law could see this profound aspect of the Good News Jesus declared:

You are not far from the Kingdom of God (12:34).

After this comment no one dared to ask any more questions (12:34; see 3:4). He had responded to every challenge. He had laid bare the true meaning of the Good News. He now takes the initiative and reinforces the teaching contained in these three passages (12:13–34).

2. Jesus Takes the Initiative, 12:35–44

OVERVIEW. These three passages roughly correspond to the three preceding passages. In each of them Jesus observes some attitude or activity and draws from it a deeper understanding of the Good News of the Kingdom.

a. David's Son, 12:35–37

The first question asked of Jesus assumed that man's relationship with God and with the emperor could be placed on the same level (12:14). Jesus responded by insisting that the Kingdom of God was on an entirely different level of human existence. Here Jesus goes further and suggests that the messiah as well cannot be conceived of as being on the same level as human kings.

The popular notion of the messiah was that he would be a descendant of David (see Jer 23:5; Ez 37:23–24; 1 Chr 7:11, 14; Dn 9:25–26). Jesus, however, quotes Ps 110:1 which was assumed to have been written by David and in which the author of the psalm speaks of the messiah as my Lord:

> *The Lord (i.e., God) said to my Lord (i.e., the messiah): Sit here at my right side, until I put your enemies under your feet (12:36).*

The question Jesus asks is not answered nor can it be answered in a simple straightforward manner:

> *how, then, can the Messiah be David's descendant (12:37)?*

This question, like other questions Jesus asks (see 9:12), is intended as an open-ended question pointing to the full reality of Jesus and the Kingdom, a reality that cannot be encompassed in the words and categories of human experience.

b. Teachers of the Law, 12:38–40

In his response to the second question Jesus had insisted that God is "the God of the living, not of the dead" (12:27). Here he points out the behavior of the teachers of the Law as examples of lives cut off from the living God.

The teachers of the Law were the professional custodians of the written Law of Moses, a law written on stone rather than on the hearts of men. The behavior of these teachers of the Law showed that they were more interested in affirming their own lives than living in God's Kingdom. Their desire to save their own lives will result in their loss of life: "Their punishment will be all the worse" (12:40)!

c. The Widow's Offering, 12:41–44

The third question asked of Jesus resulted in one teacher of the Law coming very near the Kingdom of God. He showed an understanding of the meaning of love, a perfect openness to the will of God. Mark now concludes this series of passages with the example of the widow showing, by her action, this perfect openness to God's will.

The amount she contributed to the temple treasury was insignificant compared to what others were donating. In today's economy the amount she contributed would be about fifty cents. What she does is so important, however, that Jesus speaks of it using his formula for solemn affirmation:

> *I tell you (Amen, I say to you) that this poor widow put more in*
> *the offering box than all the others. For the others put in what*
> *they had to spare of their riches; but she, poor as she is, put in*
> *all she had—she gave all she had to live on (12:43–44).*

The widow let go of herself. She gave up the very last security she had and committed herself entirely to God's mercy.

This incident marks the end of the public ministry of Jesus. From this point until his arrest Jesus is alone with the disciples. His public ministry draws to a close with the leaders of the Jews obstinately refusing to be touched by his proclamation of the Kingdom. There is, however, a ray of hope. One teacher of the Law understands the meaning of love. One poor widow surrenders all she had to live on in complete openness to the will of God.

The understanding of the teacher of the Law and the self-sacrifice of the widow serve as a prelude to Jesus' laying down his life out of obedience to God and love for mankind.

C. FINAL DISCOURSE, 13:1–37

OVERVIEW. This final public discourse of Jesus is often called the apocalyptic discourse because of the language and imagery used. The term apocalyptic refers to a special kind of literature that developed among the Jews in the final centuries before Christ. The best known example of this kind of literature is found in the book of Daniel.

God's provident control over the lives and history of his people is a constant theme throughout the Old Testament. This divine providence, however, is most difficult to see in times of extreme hardship or persecution. Times such as these gave birth to apocalyptic literature, i.e., writings that laid out a blueprint showing

God's hand in events past, present and future. The language of apocalyptic was highly symbolic but the reader could easily locate the present troubles in the apocalyptic plan and see how future events were likely to unfold. No Jew of the second century B.C. would have had any difficulty in seeing the madness of Nebuchadnezzar as a symbol of the then ruling Seleucid monarch Antiochus Epiphanes IV (Dn 4:4–33).

Mark 13, however, is not, strictly speaking, apocalyptic. It differs from apocalyptic in two important ways. First, it is not a blueprint of the future but instead places all of its emphasis on the realities of the present. As with the prophetic literature of the Old Testament, references to the future are designed to make the concerns of the present even more urgent (13:34). Second, the future that is envisioned in this discourse is not the annihilation of present enemies as in apocalyptic but rather the gathering together of all God's people (13:10, 27).

This passage was composed by Mark with a concern for the church of his day. It consists of sayings taken from Jesus' ministry, sayings which had utilized words and images from Jewish apocalyptic. Mark's concern in organizing this material was to clarify even further the already and not yet character of God's Kingdom. He was writing for a community that was experiencing suffering and persecution. He wanted to encourage them in living their Christian discipleship and to strengthen their faith.

1. Introduction, 13:1–4

Still in the third day of his entrance into Jerusalem, Jesus leaves the temple and sits on the Mount of Olives. The discourse he is about to deliver there is occasioned by his comment on the destruction of the temple, a destruction which symbolizes the end of Judaism as the point of man's contact with God (13:2). This comment will later be brought up as testimony against him at his trial (14:58) and as a source of derision as he hangs on the cross (15:29).

The subject of the discourse, however, is not the destruction of the temple but rather "all these things" (13:4). The first four disciples to have been called, those who have heard and seen everything Jesus did, want to know when "all these things" he has been teaching about will occur. Jesus will not tell them when (13:32). Instead he responds with this final discourse on discipleship, a discourse which emphasizes the already of God's Kingdom as it was being experienced by the Christians of Mark's day and also points to the not yet of the Kingdom as a source of hope and strength.

2. Present Troubles, 13:5–23

The purpose of this passage is not to provide a blueprint of what will happen but rather to describe the present experience of the church around the year 65 A.D. At that time Christians in many places were suffering persecution. The first letter of Peter addresses a similar situation:

> *Be firm in your faith and resist him (the Devil), because you know that your fellow believers in all the world are going through the same kind of sufferings (1 Pt 5:9).*

At this time in Roman history war was just breaking out in Palestine, and rumors were spreading among Christians throughout the empire about what this would mean. Apocalyptic speculation was mounting. Mark deliberately attempts to discourage this speculation.

> *They do not mean that the end has come (13:7).*

The passage begins and ends with a warning about false prophets and false messiahs (13:5–6, 21–23). Apocalyptic speculation has appeared in every age, including our own. Terrible and awesome events occur that lead some to prophesy the imminent end of the world. Such speculating, however, can only distract Christians from living their discipleship in the already of God's Kingdom.

3. The End, 13:24–27

The end will come when the time has arrived for the full reality of God's Kingdom. The end will come when the time has arrived for all people (see 13:10) to be gathered together into the one family of God. Here Mark describes the end using the apocalyptic imagery from the book of Daniel. He specifies the time of the end as "after that time of trouble" (13:24). Jesus' time of trouble was three days: "after three days he will rise to life" (8:31). The time of trouble for the disciples is indefinite but the end is equally certain.

4. Concluding Teachings, 13:28–37

Just as the image of the fig tree was used to symbolize the end of Judaism's unique role in salvation (11:14), so now the fig tree is used to symbolize the completion of all things (13:28–29). The certainty that the end will come, i.e., the not yet of God's Kingdom, is followed immediately by Mark's main emphasis in this entire passage:

> *No one knows, however, when that day or hour will come—*
> *neither the angels in heaven, nor the Son; only the Father knows.*
> *Be on watch, be alert, for you do not know when the time will be*
> *(13:32–33).*

The second half of Mark's Gospel began with an urgent call to discipleship (8:34—9:1). The last discourse of Jesus ends here with that same urgent appeal, the appeal for vigilance in the life of the church between the suffering of the Son of Man and his final return.

It is easy to be a Christian when everything is going well, when there is peace and prosperity, when conversions abound and miracles are everywhere. When things go wrong, however, our faith is put to the test. As 1 Peter expresses it:

> *My dear friends, do not be surprised at the painful test you*
> *are suffering, as though something unusual were happening*
> *to you. Rather be glad that you are sharing Christ's suffering, so*
> *that you may be full of joy when his glory is revealed (1 Pt*
> *4:12–13).*

If we truly believe that Jesus is the messiah, the suffering Son of Man, the Son of God, if we are his disciples who have left everything to carry our cross and follow him, then no matter what happens we remain with him. The urgency of this message for us is given prominence by the behavior of the disciples in the final section of the Gospel. There, when suffering becomes a reality in the life of Jesus, they desert him (14:50).

STUDY QUESTIONS

1. Is our practice of religion today open to the criticism that we do not bear fruit (11:13), or that our observances are narrow and superficial (11:17)? Do we demonstrate our belief that Jesus came to save everyone?

2. What is meant by "faith that can move mountains" (11:23)? Have we ever encountered people with that kind of faith? Do our prayers manifest that kind of faith?

3. Compare Mk 12:33 with 1 Jn 4:19–21. How can we tell if our love of God is genuine?

4. A person with family responsibilities might not be able to surrender everything as did the widow (12:44). Does her act have any meaning for the way we conduct our lives?

5. How do we respond to the crises of the present day: international instability, public acceptance of immorality, ridicule of genuine Christian living? Do these crises influence the way we understand and communicate the Good News?

6. Many Christians today understand current social and political events as pointing to the second coming of Jesus. How would Mark respond to this opinion?

Chapter Eight

PASSION, DEATH AND RESURRECTION

SUMMARY. In this final chapter we will consider the passion, death and resurrection of Jesus. Everything that Mark has written prepares us for understanding these climactic events.

The Good News of salvation is the arrival of the Kingdom of God where God's perfect will for all mankind is brought about. The death of Jesus on the cross in obedience and love is the perfect realization of God's Kingdom. By his death the Kingdom of God is displayed for all to see and entrance into it becomes possible for everyone.

We will consider, in this chapter, the events preparing for this final moment, the anointing at Bethany and the Last Supper. We will consider the varied behavior and responses of the many characters Mark describes during these final hours, e.g., Simon Peter who denies Jesus and Simon of Cyrene who carries his cross.

We will conclude by considering the new life that Jesus has won for us. We will ponder the meaning of the empty tomb and prepare to follow Jesus as he goes before us into Galilee.

READ 14:1–16:8

OVERVIEW. As Mark has unfolded for us the Good News of salvation we have seen quite opposite developments in Jesus on the one hand and in his disciples on the other. As the true identity of Jesus unfolded we saw Jesus, in his words and deeds, being uncompromisingly true to his identify. In this final section we will see the Son of God dying in obedience to his Father and in commitment to the service of others. When Jesus first proclaimed the Kingdom of God the disciples failed to understand him. When he focused on his own identify as the one in whom the Kingdom of God is first realized, the disciples' lack of understanding changed to positive misunderstanding. Now, as the true nature of God's Kingdom becomes perfectly clear in the climactic events of Jesus' life, the disciples will desert him.

Other characters will appear in this section to provide a refreshing contrast to the behavior of the disciples. There are the women: the one who anoints Jesus in anticipation of the fulfillment of his mission and several who do not, like the disciples, flee, but who remain to observe Jesus' death and burial. It is they who discover the empty tomb. There is also Simon of Cyrene who fulfills the call to discipleship by actually carrying Jesus' cross. Most importantly there is the Roman soldier who recognizes the full reality of who Jesus is and what he accomplishes.

A. ANOINTING AND EUCHARIST, 14:1–31

OVERVIEW. Both the anointing at Bethany and the Last Supper are presented as symbols of what will happen. The anointing is a symbol of Jesus' burial while the Last Supper is a symbol of his sacrifice on the cross. Both symbols are inserted by Mark into other preliminary material. The symbol of burial is inserted within two sections of the plot to kill Jesus. The symbol of crucifixion is inserted within two accounts of Jesus' predictions about his disciples reaction to his relentless movement toward death.

1. Anticipation of Death and Burial, 14:1–11

a. Betrayal, 14:1–2, 10–11

That Jesus will die is certain. How he will die remains to be worked out. How people will respond to his death remains to be seen. Here, at the beginning of the final section of his Gospel,

Mark explains how the death of Jesus came about. He sets this account in proper perspective, however, by using it to frame a far more important incident, an incident in which the true meaning of Jesus' death was understood and appreciated (14:3–9).

Two days before the Feast of Passover, i.e., on Wednesday, the leaders of the Jews have decided to arrest and kill Jesus (14:1). Earlier we were told that they had wanted to kill him (11:18), and on another occasion that they had decided to arrest him (12:12). Now their plan is crystal-clear. They will arrest him secretly and then put him to death (14:1).

The Feast of Passover would bring an additional two hundred thousand people to a city with a normal population of about fifty thousand. Any disturbance could spark a riot that would be brutally suppressed by the Romans. Jesus' arrest could trigger such a disturbance, for many of the people, especially the visitors from Galilee, regarded Jesus as a possible messiah. The Jewish leaders, then, needed to find a way to arrest Jesus quietly. Judas provides for their needs (14:10).

Why Judas decided to betray Jesus we do not know. Unlike John, who suggests that Judas was greedy (Jn 12:4–6), Mark nowhere provides a motive. He does indicate that it was God's will that Jesus be betrayed. At the same time, however, Jesus' judgment on Judas' behavior is far more severe then on the other eleven who desert him (14:21).

b. Anointing at Bethany, 14:3–9

The practice of pouring perfume over a person's head may seem strange to us but was, in Jesus' day, a proper and acceptable form of hospitality. This practice is what is referred to in Psalm 133:

> *Behold, how good and pleasant it is when brothers dwell in unity! It is like the precious oil upon the head, running down upon the beard, upon the beard of Aaron (Ps 133:1–2).*

An unidentified woman pours a large amount of precious perfume over Jesus' head (14:3). The value of this perfume in the economy of the time was equivalent to what a laborer could earn in a year (14:5). Some of the onlookers criticized her for being wasteful, prompting a reply from Jesus. (The format is that of a pronouncement story.)

Jesus maintains that "she has done a fine and beautiful thing" (14:6) and gives three reasons, all of which point to an awareness of what would soon happen to Jesus. First, she recognized that this was the last time she could do anything for Jesus (14:7). She was not unconcerned for the poor but did recognize the tremendous importance of Jesus and the unique opportunity to respond to his presence. So often people become so preoccupied with the ordinary affairs of their lives that unique opportunities are missed; unique moments of grace are ignored.

Second, she actually prepared Jesus' body for its burial (14:8). Because the Jewish Sabbath would begin at sundown on the day of Jesus' death there would be no time to anoint his body. Other women will return on Sunday to anoint the body but the tomb will be empty. This woman, then, by doing "what she could" (14:8) was actually providing Jesus with his pre-burial anointing. In the Kingdom of God the ultimate success of our deeds is in the hands of God. All we can do or be expected to do is respond to the grace of the moment. Jesus' praise for this woman is similar to the praise he had for the widow in the temple who "gave all she had" (12:44).

Finally, using his solemn affirmation formula, he praises the woman because what she has done not only anticipates his death but anticipates as well the worldwide proclamation of the Gospel. Jesus' death in obedience and love makes the Kingdom of God available to all. This woman prepares Jesus for his death, already manifesting in her actions his obedience and his love. Her love and her insight stand in sharp contrast to the conspiring authorities of Judaism (14:1–2, 10–11).

2. Anticipation of Arrest and Crucifixion, 14:12–31

a. Preparation, 14:12–16

The day before Passover, Thursday, was the day the lambs for the Passover meal were slaughtered (14:12). All the work for the

Passover meal had to be completed before sundown on this day. This passage (14:12–16) sets the scene for the second great anticipatory event, the Last Supper. Mark deliberately structures this preparatory passage to parallel the preparations for Jesus' entry into Jerusalem.

Mark 11	Mark 14
[1] Jesus sent two of his disciples on ahead	[13] Jesus sent two of them out
[2] with these instructions, "Go to the village . . .	with these instructions: [14] "Go into the city . . .
[3] . . . tell him, 'The Master needs. . . .' "	. . . say to the owner . . . 'The Teacher says. . . .' "
[4] they went and found a colt. . . .	[16] . . . went to the city, and found everything. . . .

Here, as in his entry into Jerusalem, Jesus is deliberately setting out on a course that will lead to suffering and death. He knows full well what lies ahead. The disciples in both cases follow his instructions but misunderstand the real significance of what he is doing.

b. Predictions, 14:17–21, 27–31

In these passages the behavior of the disciples is used to frame the passage on the Eucharist, the symbol of Jesus' redemptive act on the cross. The leaders of the Jews sought to arrest and kill Jesus. The symbolic anticipation of his death, then, is framed by predictions about what one disciple will do to bring about his arrest and how the remainder will react as a result of his arrest.

The last three solemn affirmations of Mark's Gospel occur in these passages (14:18, 25, 30). The first concerns the betrayer, the last concerns Peter.

(Amen, I say to you) one of you will betray me—one who is eating with me (14:18).

(Amen, I say to you) before the rooster crows two times tonight, you will say three times that you do not know me (14:30).

What is most striking about the two predictions is the enormous difference in Jesus' attitude. To those who run away and leave Jesus he says:

After I am raised to life I will go to Galilee ahead of you (14:28)

Concerning the one who betrays him, however, his remarks are totally different:

How terrible for that man who will betray the Son of Man! It would have been better for that man if he had never been born (14:21).

What we have here is a specific application of a principle laid down in the very first solemn affirmation in Mark's Gospel:

(Amen, I say to you!) Men can be forgiven all their sins and all the evil things they may say. But whoever says evil things against the Holy Spirit will never be forgiven, because he has committed an eternal sin (3:28–29).

The one who betrays Jesus has closed his mind and heart to the reality of God's Kingdom. His is not a sin of human weakness but a sin of blasphemy.

The remainder of the disciples will fail just as it is written in the book of Zechariah:

Strike the shepherd, that the sheep may be scattered (Zech 13:7).

Sheep are totally dependent on their shepherd for survival. Without the shepherd sheep cannot find food or drink or shelter. They are helpless. The disciples will be rendered as helpless as stranded sheep. In that very helplessness, however, the true nature of discipleship will be brought out. Christian discipleship is possible only because Jesus has gone ahead, only because Jesus has first suffered, died and risen. The disciples will be scattered momentarily, but after Jesus is raised he will go ahead of them into Galilee (14:28; see 1:39; 16:7).

c. Eucharist, 14:22–26

The Passover meal was eaten every year as a remembrance of the liberation from Egypt. The first time it was eaten the people were instructed to eat it with sandals on their feet and staff in hand (Ex 12:11; see Mk 6:8–9). They were to be ready to set out on a journey into the unknown, led by God. This final Passover meal, eaten by Jesus and his disciples, becomes a symbol of man's liberation from every kind of bondage. Jesus here shares with his disciples the full meaning of what he will accomplish on the cross.

In the Semitic understanding the term "body" meant much more than the flesh as opposed to the blood. It meant the entire being, physical as well as mental. It referred to the whole person. What Jesus means by the words "this is my body" (14:22) is that his entire person is being given to nourish those who follow him.

The significance of blood is however, somewhat different from that of body. We read in Leviticus:

> *The life of every creature is the blood of it; therefore I have said to the people of Israel, You shall not eat the blood of any creature, for the life of every creature is in its blood; whoever eats it shall be cut off (Lv 17:14).*

Blood is the bearer of life. Jesus will pour out his life on the cross so that all mankind can share in that life (see 10:45). At the Last Supper, then, Jesus shares his entire being with his disciples and allows them to drink his very life.

His final comment, a solemn affirmation, sets the eucharistic meal in an even broader context:

> *(Amen, I say to you) I will never again drink this wine until the day I drink the new wine in the Kingdom of God (14:25).*

This comment is primarily an assurance to the disciples that the messianic banquet, into which Jesus had just initiated them, would continue. For Jesus, however, this comment was a firm commitment to the cup of suffering he must now drink (see

10:38). He makes this commitment with the clear conviction that after his period of suffering he will rise to drink anew the life of God's Kingdom.

B. SUFFERING AND DEATH, 14:32–15:39

OVERVIEW: This passage which details the definitive event in the history of salvation is presented in four scenes: Gethsemane (14:32–52), the High Priest's house (14:53–72), Pilate's residence (15:1–21), and Golgotha (15:22–39). In each of these scenes Jesus utters one crucial saying:

[1] My Father! All things are possible for you. Take this cup from me. But not what I want, but what you want (14:36).

[2] The High Priest questioned him, "Are you the Messiah, the Son of the Blessed God?" "I am," answered Jesus, "and you will see the Son of Man coming with the clouds of heaven" (14:61–62)!

[3] Pilate questioned him, "Are you the king of the Jews?" Jesus answered, "So you say" (15:2).

[4] My God, my God, why did you abandon me (15:34)?

The sayings of Jesus in each of these scenes, sayings which are revelatory of his identity and mission, are complemented by the reactions of four different individuals at the end of each of these scenes. After the arrest in Gethsemane a young follower of Jesus will run away naked (14:51–52). After Jesus' condemnation by the Sanhedrin Peter will deny Jesus three times (14:66–72). After his sentencing by Pilate a stranger from Cyrene will carry Jesus' cross (15:21–22). After his death on the cross a Roman soldier will recognize his full identity as Son of God (15:39).

1. Gethsemane, 14:32–50

a. Jesus Prays, 14:32–41

Gethsemane was the site of an olive grove on the slope of the Mount of Olives facing Jerusalem. After the supper Jesus goes there with his disciples to pray. Mark records only three occasions in Jesus' life when he prayed: after the first day of his healing ministry (1:35), after he nourished the five thousand (6:46), and after he gave his own body and blood to his disciples (14:32). Each time Jesus had given of himself in the service of others, the final self-giving involving his entire person, his very life. The symbolic self-giving of the Eucharist is about to be realized on the cross. Here in the garden, for the first time in Mark's Gospel, we see the content of Jesus' prayer, the manner in which he opened himself to the will of his Father.

For the third and final time Jesus brings with him his three closest disciples to witness this moment of intimacy with the Father (14:33; see 5:37; 9:2). They had seen his glory on the mountain of the transfiguration; now they are invited to see his agony and his human weakness. Since the anointing at Bethany Jesus' suffering had been increasing. Now it is so great that it almost crushes him (14:34). No one has as yet laid a hand on him but there is a growing realization of abandonment. Anyone who has experienced the pain of loneliness knows it can be far more severe than any physical pain. In this moment of intense loneliness Jesus brings his three closest companions but even they fail him. Three times he turns to his Father in prayer; three times he returns to his three disciples; each time they are asleep (14:35–41).

In the Kingdom of God everyone does the will of God. Only once before in Mark's Gospel, however, was the will of God explicitly mentioned:

> *Whoever does what God wants him to do is my brother, my sister, my mother (3:35)!*

Here in the garden Jesus realizes that no one is doing what God wants. Jesus is alone. It is easy to be good when everyone around you is good. It is another matter entirely when you stand all alone in your desire to be virtuous. Jesus, in the depths of his humanity, felt the tension between what God expected of him and what he could endure all by himself. His prayer expresses the fullness of the humanity he shares with us as well as a perfect commitment to the will of God:

> *My Father! All things are possible for you. Take this cup away from me. But not what I want, but what you want (14:36).*

b. Arrest, 14:41–52

When Jesus finishes praying he awakens the disciples for the third time and declares:

> *The hour has come (14:41).*

Jesus' entire life had been moving relentlessly toward this hour. He predicted with ever increasing clarity the events of this hour. In spite of the suffering involved he vigorously affirmed the will of God and arrived at the hour for which God had sent him.

In his third prediction (10:33–34) he had said that he would be handed over to the leaders of the Jews who would in turn hand him over to the Gentiles. Here he recognizes his betrayer, the one who hands him over to the Jewish leaders (14:42). In the dark of night Jesus could be arrested without causing a disturbance. Ju-

das' function was to locate him in the dark and identify him. He carries out his betrayal with a kiss (14:45).

As Jesus had predicted, one of the twelve betrays him and the other eleven "left him and ran away" (14:50). In following his destiny Jesus finds himself alone, separated from his enemies by hostility and from his friends by desertion.

The story of the arrest concludes with the curious incident about the naked young man (14:51–52). This incident is the only one in Mark's passion narrative that is ignored by all three of the other Gospel writers. Commentators from earliest times have wondered who this person was and why Mark included this incident. Some modern commentators have suggested that the young man might have been Mark himself. What is more likely, however, is that Mark uses this incident in much the same way he uses the incident about Simon of Cyrene, i.e., to conclude a scene with a character whose behavior illustrates the meaning of that scene. The naked young man emphasizes the fact that not only the disciples but everyone who might have been a supporter of Jesus deserted him and fled.

2. High Priest's House, 14:53–72

a. Jesus before the Sanhedrin, 14:53–65

Jesus was brought before the assembly of the chief priests, elders and teachers of the Law. The Sanhedrin, as it was called, had wide jurisdiction over religious and civic matters. Certain affairs, however, were reserved to the Roman authorities such as carrying out a death sentence. The proceedings of the Sanhedrin were carried on according to Jewish law which specified, among other things, that

> *a single witness shall not prevail against a man for any crime or for any wrong in connection with any offense that he has committed; only on the evidence of two witnesses, or of three witnesses, shall a charge be sustained (Dt 19:15).*

The Sanhedrin, however, was unable to find two or more witnesses who could agree on any charge, even the charge resulting from a misinterpretation of Jesus' prediction about the end of the temple (14:57–59; see 13:2).

Throughout the proceedings Jesus remained silent. Here and elsewhere Mark is deliberately presenting Jesus as the suffering servant of Deutero-Isaiah:

> He was oppressed, and he was afflicted, yet he opened not his mouth; like a lamb that is led to the slaughter, and like a sheep that before its shearers is dumb, so he opened not his mouth (Is 53:7).

Jesus does, however, speak once and only once in this trial, as he will in the subsequent trial before Pilate. In both instances he responds to a question about his identity. Jesus will not die because of anything he said or because of anything he did. He will die because of who he is. He is God's Son.

The leaders of the Jews, however, refuse to acknowledge any point of contact between God and man other than that over which they exercise control. When the High Priest asks him if he is the Messiah, the Son of the Blessed God, Jesus responds as he had responded to Peter at Caesarea Philippi (8:31) with a corrective statement about the Son of Man:

> I am, and you will see the Son of Man seated at the right side of the Almighty, and coming with the clouds of heaven (14:62).

To presume to sit at God's right hand, like presuming to be able to forgive sins (2:7), is blasphemy, a crime punishable by death. Actually, by refusing to acknowledge the power of God in Jesus, it is the Sanhedrin that is guilty of blasphemy (see 3:29). They, however, cannot see their error and by unanimous vote condemn Jesus to death. The final verse in this passage (14:65) again recalls the suffering servant:

> He was wounded for our transgressions, he was bruised for our iniquities (Is 53:5).

b. Peter's Denial, 14:66–72

When Jesus was arrested everyone, including the naked young man, deserted him. Now, when Jesus is courageously true to his identity as Son of God, Peter denies his own identity as a disciple of Jesus. The three denials show a clear progression from pretended ignorance (14:68) to a simple denial (14:69) to a denial accompanied with an oath (14:71).

Jesus' faithfulness stands in stark contrast to man's unfaithfulness. The enormity of Peter's failure suddenly dawns on him when he hears the rooster crow and remembers Jesus' prediction (14:72). He cries.

3. Pilate's Residence, 15:1–21

Being unable to carry out a death sentence, the Sanhedrin, early on Friday morning, brings Jesus to Pilate, the Roman governor (15:1). As Jesus had predicted, the Sanhedrin has handed him over to Gentiles (10:33). Jesus again refuses to speak except to answer one question "Are you the king of the Jews" (15:2)? Jesus responds with a half-hearted "So you say" (15:2).

From Pilate's perspective Jesus had committed no crime at all (15:14). Pilate was like a colonial governor with nothing but disdain for the tribal superstitions of the native people. If the chief priests were upset by a man claiming to be the messiah or the Son of Man, Pilate certainly was not. Pilate actually wanted to set Jesus free (15:9).

The chief priests, however, were determined to force Pilate to execute Jesus. A crowd had gathered at Pilate's residence, not because of Jesus (he had arrived secretly) but because of Pilate's custom of freeing a prisoner on the Feast of Passover (15:6). Pilate tried to use the crowd to secure Jesus' freedom but the chief priests had already instigated the crowd to demand his crucifixion (15:9–13). They chose instead a murderer named Barabbas (15:11).

As Mark presents the story the responsibility for Jesus' execution rests clearly with the Jewish leaders. Judas had handed Jesus over to them, and the Romans will carry out his execution but it is the Jewish leaders who manipulate Judas, Pilate and the crowd in securing the crucifixion of Jesus.

This trial ends as the previous one did with Jesus being mocked and abused (15:16–20; see 14:65). The Roman soldiers probably had no personal animosity toward Jesus but seem to have subjected him to much greater physical abuse than did the Jewish guards after the first trial. By the time he was led out to be crucified he was so weakened that he was unable to carry his cross.

After the passion prediction Jesus had said:

> *If anyone wants to come with me he must forget himself,* carry
> his cross, *and* follow me *(8:34).*

The young man in the garden of Gethsemane was "following Jesus . . . but he ran away naked" (14:51–52). The High Priest's servant said to Peter: "You, too, were with Jesus" (14:67), but Peter denied it. Now a total stranger is called upon to carry Jesus' cross.

Cyrene was a city in what is now the country of Libya. It had a significant Jewish population, and Simon was probably one of these Jews from Cyrene who had come to Jerusalem for the feast. Simon of Cyrene is the third Simon to appear in the three final days of Jesus' life. On Wednesday Jesus was in the house of Simon the leper when the woman anointed him (14:3). On Thursday Jesus is in the garden of Gethsemane when he criticizes Peter with the words: "Simon, are you asleep?" (14:37). (Peter had not been referred to as Simon since we were told his name had been changed in 3:16, nor will he be so referred to again.) Now on Friday a third Simon, a total stranger, carries Jesus' cross while all the disciples have fled.

4. Crucifixion, 15:22–39

The final moments of Jesus' life reflect the image presented in Psalm 69:

> *Insults have broken my heart so that I am in despair.*
> *I looked for pity, but there was none; and for comforters, but I*
> *found none.*

They gave me poison for food, and for my thirst they gave me vinegar to drink (Ps 69:20–21).

The event at Golgotha begins with an attempt to poison Jesus (15:23) and ends with an offer of vinegar (15:36). Wine mixed with myrrh was a drug used to alleviate pain. Jesus chooses to face his final moment in full possession of his senses (15:23). A cheap thirst-quencher used by the poor was sour wine mixed with water (15:36). Even this Jesus refuses, for he had said the night before:

I will never again drink this wine until the day I drink the new wine in the Kingdom of God (14:25)

The events which Mark recounts in these final moments fulfill the words of Psalm 22 with the order reversed:

Ps 22	Mk 14
16. They have pierced my hands and my feet.	24. Then they nailed him to the cross and divided his clothes among themselves, throwing dice to see who would get each piece of clothing.
17. I can count all my bones—they stare and gloat over me;	
18. they divide my garments among them, and for my raiment they cast lots.	
7. All who see me mock at me, they make mouths at me, they wag their heads.	29. People passing by shook their heads and hurled insults at Jesus.
8. He committed his cause to the Lord; let him deliver him.	31. He saved others but he cannot save himself.
1. My God, my God, why hast thou forsaken me?	34. My God, my God, why did you abandon me?

Crucifixion was described by Cicero as the "most cruel and repulsive of punishments." People hung for hours writhing in agony while the last drops of life's energy drained from their bodies. Jesus refused to accept any amelioration of his suffering and instead remained true to his dignity as God's Son to the end. Even in his humiliation, dignity was displayed in the inscription.

> *The King of the Jews (15:26).*

It was the custom to display publicly the reason for a person's execution. Pilate ordered this inscription both as a statement of his understanding of the charges brought against Jesus and as a display of his contempt for the leaders of the Jews. In addition, however, this notice served to point to the far deeper reality of who this person really was.

All those present at the cross mocked and insulted Jesus—the leaders of the Jews, people passing by, even the two criminals crucified with him. Concerning people such as these Paul wrote:

> *The message about Christ's death on the cross is nonsense to those who are being lost; but for us who are being saved, it is God's power (1 Cor 1:18).*

The leaders of the Jews, those chiefly responsible for bringing Jesus to the cross, offer to believe in him if he will come down from the cross (15:32). Again Jesus is being asked for a sign (see 8:11); again he is being tempted. Jesus, however, does nothing and says nothing. He hangs in quiet dignity for three hours bearing their insults (from 9 A.M. until noon) and for another three hours while darkness covered the earth (15:33).

Darkness was a sign that signaled the day of judgment. The prophet Joel had written:

> *The sun shall be turned to darkness, and the moon to blood, before the great and terrible day of the Lord comes (Jl 2:31).*

In his final discourse Jesus had used the same imagery to describe the coming of the Son of Man:

> *In the days after that time of trouble the sun will grow dark, the moon will no longer shine (13:24).*

Now as Jesus hangs on the cross that moment has finally arrived when God's will would be perfectly fulfilled in the death of his Son. The final moment in the history of mankind has arrived. Jesus signals this moment with the only words he speaks from the cross:

My God, my God, why did you abandon me (15:34)?

The totality of his suffering, his total abandonment, is accompanied by a final perfect acknowledgment of the will of God. The perfection of the Kingdom of God, here present, is subject, however, to one final misunderstanding. They think he is calling for Elijah (15:36; see 9:11–13).

With a cry of pain Jesus dies (15:37). At that moment the curtain of the temple is torn in two (15:38). Judaism's claim to hold exclusive access to God is ended. Access to God is now available only through the death of Jesus. As the author of the letter to the Hebrews wrote:

We have, then, brothers, complete freedom to go into the Most Holy Place by means of the death of Jesus. He opened for us a new way, a living way, through the curtain—that is, through his own body (Heb 10:19–20).

As the exclusive role of Judaism is ended, as the new life of God's Kingdom is made available to all, it is a Gentile, a Roman soldier, who becomes the first human to recognize the full reality of who Jesus is and what he has accomplished for us:

This man was really the Son of God (15:39).

C. BURIAL AND RESURRECTION, 15:40—16:8

1. Burial, 15:40–47

The story of Jesus' burial is framed by the account of women watching from a distance. Women occupied a very low position in both Jewish and pagan society. When everyone else has fled, however, it is the women who remain. They are at a safe distance, but they remain. They see Jesus die; they see Jospeh take his body; they see where he is buried.

The story of the burial is a simple account confirming the reality of Jesus' death. Joseph of Arimathea obeys the law regarding executed criminals:

> *His body shall not remain all night upon the tree, but you shall*
> *bury him the same day, for a hanged man is accursed by God*
> *(Dt 21:23).*

The burial was hasty because as soon as the sun set it would be the Jewish Sabbath. There was no time for the customary anointing of the body. It was merely laid in a rock-hewn tomb and the entrance closed with a large stone.

2. Resurrection, 16:1–8

The actual resurrection of Jesus is not described by Mark nor is it described anywhere in the New Testament. It is not described because it cannot be described. The resurrection of Jesus is not an ordinary human event that can be described in ordinary human language. Jesus' resurrection is not simply the undoing of his death, the restoration of the life he had before his death. It is, instead, an entrance into a totally new kind of life, a kind of life that we who have been baptized share.

The women who saw Jesus' hasty burial on Friday afternoon wait until Saturday evening, when the Sabbath is over, to buy the necessary spices (16:1). Early on Sunday morning as they approach the tomb they ask a very human question:

> *Who will roll away for us the stone (16:3)?*

Their question is similar to the disciples' question after the incident with the rich man:

> *Who, then, can be saved (10:26)?*

God's ways, however, are not man's ways. Something totally new in human experience has happened. The stone is already rolled away. The anguish of the cross has yielded to the mystery of the empty tomb.

A young man wearing a white robe (a symbol of heavenly being) explains the meaning of the empty tomb and tells the women to give the message to the disciples that Jesus is going ahead of them to Galilee (16:6–7). Do the women understand? Do they report to the disciples? Mark does not tell us!

The empty tomb is the final parabolic incident in Mark's Gospel. Its meaning cannot be explained in ordinary human language. Its meaning can only be grasped by those who already have a faith relationship with Jesus. The Jewish leaders will later claim that the disciples stole the body of Jesus. Even today we hear speculation that Jesus was not really dead but only drugged in such a way as to appear dead.

The women's immediate response to the empty tomb is fear and terror (16:8). Here Mark's Gospel ends. It ends where it began with the open-ended symbol of Galilee (see 1:39). The Good News of God's Kingdom goes before us into all the world. How do we respond to the empty tomb?

STUDY QUESTIONS

1. The woman at Bethany responded to a unique opportunity to do what she could (14:8). How could we be better prepared to recognize and respond to such opportunities in our lives?

2. The disciples deserted Jesus because they were weak. Do we notice similar weaknesses in ourselves?

3. Which of the events of Jesus' passion has the greatest impact on my own life?

4. What do you think the centurion saw or experienced that led him to exclaim, "This man was really the Son of God" (15:39)?

5. Why can the resurrection of Jesus not be understood merely as a restoration to his former physical life?

6. Mark's Gospel ends with the fear and terror of the women (16:8). Do we appreciate why they felt as they did? How do we now feel about the Good News of salvation?

Appendix

Chapter One: Daily Study Assignment

Day	Mark
1	1:1–8
2	1:9–13
3	1:14–15
4	1:16–34
5	1:35–39

6—Reflect on 1:1–39 in light of the reflection questions listed at the end of the chapter.

7—STUDY GROUP MEETING

Chapter Two: Daily Study Assignment

Day	Mark
1	1:40–45
2	2:1–12
3	2:13–22
4	2:23–28
5	3:1–6

6—Reflect on 1:40—3:6 in light of the reflection questions listed at the end of the chapter.

7—STUDY GROUP MEETING

Chapter Three: Daily Study Assignment

Day	Mark
1	3:7–19
2	3:20–35
3	4:1–34
4	4:35—5:20
5	5:21–6:6

6—Reflect on 3:7—6:6 in light of the reflection questions listed at the end of the chapter.

7—STUDY GROUP MEETING

Chapter Four: Daily Study Assignment

Day	Mark
1	6:6–29
2	6:30–56
3	7:1–23
4	7:24–37
5	8:1–26

6—Reflect on 6:6—8:26 in light of the reflection questions listed and the end of the chapter.

7—STUDY GROUP MEETING

Chapter Five: Daily Study Assignment

Day	Mark
1	8:27–30
2	8:31–33
3	8:34—9:1
4	9:2–13
5	9:14–29

6—Reflect on 8:27—9:29 in light of the reflection questions listed at the end of the chapter.

7—STUDY GROUP MEETING

Chapter Six: Daily Study Assignment

Day	Mark
1	9:30–37
2	9:38–50
3	10:1–16
4	10:17–31
5	10:32–52

6—Reflect on 9:30—10:52 in light of the reflection questions listed at the end of the chapter.
7—STUDY GROUP MEETING

Chapter Seven: Daily Study Assignment

Day	Mark
1	11:1–19
2	11:20—12:12
3	12:13–34
4	12:35–44
5	13:1–37

6—Reflect on chapters 11 through 13 in light of the reflection questions listed at the end of the chapter.
7—STUDY GROUP MEETING

Chapter Eight: Daily Study Assignment

Day	Mark
1	14:1–11
2	14:12–31
3	14:32–72
4	15:1–39
5	15:40—16:8

6—Reflect on chapters 14 through 16 in light of the reflection questions listed at the end of the chapter.
7—STUDY GROUP MEETING